Mormons Believe ... *What?!*

Fact and Fiction About a Rising Religion

Gary C. Lawrence

Author of *How Americans View Mormonism*

The Parameter Foundation

Orange County, California

© 2011 by Gary C. Lawrence

Published by
The Parameter Foundation
PO Box 2883
Orange, CA 92859-0883
714 667 0850
www.parameterfoundation.org
www.mormonsbelievewhat.com
www.howamericansviewmormonism.com

ISBN-10: 0-9820391-2-3

ISBN-13: 978-0-9820391-2-0

Printed in the United States of America

To my family

Jan, Stephanie, Ben, Kristen, Matthew,
Lindsey, Ben, Abigail, Isabelle, Chase, and Fiona

CONTENTS

PART I: ANSWERS ABOUT BELIEFS

PART I: ANSWERS ABOUT PEOPLE

Acknowledgements

My thanks to the many people who assisted in the crafting of this book:

- My wife, Jan, for her love, kindness, and patience.

- My family and extended family for their encouragement.

- Ron Stone for the idea of this book.

- Hal Wing for his material support and enthusiasm.

- Karen Watts, my editor, for asking the right questions, suggesting other points of view, and catching my mistakes.

- GG and David Vandagriff for consulting and counsel.

- Scott and Maurine Proctor for giving LDS writers a voice in *Meridian Magazine*. Portions of chapters 16, 18, and 20 originally appeared in their magazine's ldsmag.com website.

- Daniel Peterson who started the MormonScholarsTestify.org website and invited me to contribute. My response became the basis for Chapter 14.

- Lisa Adair and her research team at Opinionology for their professional interviewing on my surveys.

- Colleen Bedford, my assistant, for her organizational skills, editing, and proofing, and for keeping me on track.

- Ben Rancie for book and cover layout.

- Friends too numerous to mention for their encouragement and suggestions.

And my thanks to my ancestors William Lawrence, John Armstrong, David Caldwell, and James Allred, who, in the 1800s, had the courage against much opposition to be the first in these family lines to join The Church of Jesus Christ of Latter-day Saints.

Introduction

Reading about someone else's religion is like attending a stranger's family reunion.

People are talking about Aunt Matilda or Uncle Fred, and telling stories so familiar that some cousin mutters a phrase and the place erupts in laughter or begins weeping. And you feel like a hamburger at a Hindu wedding.

The reunion is complicated because there's another group nearby and those people want a food fight.

My goal with this book is to explain to you, the observer on the sidelines, what the family reunion is all about and why those other people are lobbing pies at us.

Facts and Opinions

It begins with a simple axiom:

> People have a right to their own opinions about Mormonism, but they do not have a right to their own facts.

I study those opinions because I'm a pollster. I know the facts because I'm a Mormon.

Over my 40-year career in public opinion research, I have heard in focus groups and measured in surveys the perceptions Americans hold of Mormons – our supposed beliefs, practices, and intentions. A few get it right; most do not.

In moderating numerous focus groups where participants did not know my religious affiliation, I heard many skewed perceptions and misinformation about Mormons. One – that we are not Christians – made me want to blurt out, "What part of our name don't you understand?"

As a neutral moderator, I had to stifle the question. As an author, I saw in it a new way to explain things.

A Mormon Moment?

Curiosity about Mormonism is increasing. For the first time in history, as we go to press, two Mormons – Mitt Romney and Jon Huntsman, Jr. – are vying for the Republican presidential nomination. Today there are also Mormon political figures on both sides of the aisle, TV personalities, business leaders and gurus, athletes, *American Idol* finalists, sci-fi and vampire novelists, a Broadway musical, and perhaps a Mormon who just moved into your neighborhood. (Toss in a couple of former Miss Americas, a Jeopardy champ, and Butch Cassidy, and this family reunion might be interesting after all.)

Then there's the publicity from ministers who preach anti-Mormon sermons. But, hey, we were driven out of New York, Ohio, Missouri, and Illinois in the 1800s, and almost out of Utah, so we're used to it.

With our growing visibility comes an increase in questions, and that's where this book fits in. I hope it provides the answers you're looking for. Many who read it will disagree with our beliefs, of course, and that's okay. My objective is not to persuade, but simply to explain clearly what we Mormons believe and do not believe, and shed a little light on the reasons why.

Polling Results

To add specific insights to my narrative, I had my polling firm conduct a national public opinion survey of 1000 randomly chosen adults

July 6-13, 2011. The results are incorporated into the various chapters, with a special chapter that examines the 2012 presidential race as it intersects with religious issues. I also draw on a similar national survey my firm conducted in 2008 that formed the basis for my previous book, *How Americans View Mormonism*. The data presented in this book come from one of those two studies unless otherwise noted.

The Pies

Criticisms provide useful springboards for conversations. I proceed from the premise that a response to a criticism ("You are not a Christian!") brings out more robust and interesting insights than an answer to a question ("Are you a Christian?").

Happily, for my purposes, there are plenty of criticisms and misinformation to work with – lots of different-flavored pies being thrown. Distorted perceptions about Mormons have not faded in past years despite easy access to accurate information, and the put-downs about us are doozies:

> Mormons aren't Christians.
> Mormons don't believe the Bible.
> Mormons believe Jesus and Satan are brothers.
> Mormons practice polygamy.
> Mormons are a cult.
> Mormons are blind followers.
> Mormons believe they can work their way into heaven.
> Mormons don't believe in the Trinity.
> Mormons do weird things in their temples.
> Mormons wear magic underwear.
> Mormons treat women as second-class citizens.
> Mormons want to control the government.
> And many others.

Among these are outright falsehoods, honest misconceptions, and some that contain a kernel of truth but have been exaggerated for purpose of ridicule. I have built this book around two dozen of my favorites.

Each chapter title echoes a criticism I have personally heard or read. I respond with a short observation and then lay out the Mormon position and rationale.

That said, let me reassure you: I respect the right of every individual to believe and worship as he or she wishes. I believe every religion is healthier for having to defend its beliefs in the public square and that robust disagreement over scriptural interpretation is as American as the First Amendment.

But when civil disagreement about beliefs gives way to purposeful untruths and hurtful accusations, fair play requires that observers on the sidelines hear not only clear, thoughtful explanations, but also vigorous rebuttals.

This book contains both.

The Faith Family Distortion

Many misperceptions of Mormons can be traced to one false assumption – that there is a Mormon faith community that encompasses the 150 or so groups that have broken away from The Church of Jesus Christ of Latter-day Saints since its founding in 1830. Far too many people are under the impression that all of the splinter groups that broke away, including those that practice polygamy today, can be classified as Mormons.

Wrong.

Such groups are no more part of the Mormon faith family than Protestants are part of Catholicism. Many Americans, however, lump members of the LDS Church together with these breakaway groups.

When asked in my survey, only three in ten got it right:

> In your mind, does the word 'Mormons' refer to… only the members of The Church of Jesus Christ of Latter-day Saints … or … to all churches and groups that believe the Book of Mormon?

Only members of the LDS Church	30%
All believers in the Book of Mormon	45
No opinion	25

I believe this is a significant contributor to the Mormon image problem. The non-Mormon breakaway groups that practice polygamy number less than 100,000 while true Mormons who do not practice polygamy number over 14,000,000. The publicity is not proportional.

Given Mormonism's growing profile in American culture and the public's curiosity about our faith, it is more important than ever to make clear that we are a single-denomination faith family and the only religion that can legitimately claim the Mormon name. That is why I use the terms Mormons and the LDS Church interchangeably. They are the same.

Thank you for your interest in sorting fact from fiction about Mormonism. I will try to avoid jargon and I hope I'm not preachy on topics that require detail.

And if there are any Uncle Fred stories, I'll explain them.

Gary C. Lawrence
Orange County, California
Summer, 2011

A Short Overview of Beliefs

Here is a shorthand version of Mormonism by which to judge how close a Mormon's religious beliefs come to one's own. These key points of doctrine should help define and clarify the beliefs of The Church of Jesus Christ of Latter-day Saints.

1. We believe in God, Jesus Christ, and the Holy Ghost.

2. We believe this Godhead consists of three separate Beings. We do not believe in the Trinity description of them as found in the 4th-century creeds.

3. We believe God is the Father of our spirits and that we lived with Him in heaven before being born in our earthly bodies.

4. We believe Jesus Christ is the literal Son of God who died on the cross and on the third day was resurrected.

5. We believe all mankind will be saved from the permanence of death and will be resurrected because of Christ's atoning death and His resurrection.

6. Birth is when the spirit enters the body. Death is when it leaves. Resurrection is when the spirit is reunited with the physical body in a glorified state that is free from sickness, pain, and death.

7. We believe all mankind will live forever.

8. We believe it is by the grace of Christ that we are saved from our sins through repentance and keeping His commandments.

9. Because of Christ's atonement for Adam's transgression, we reject the concept of original sin. All babies are born sinless. Therefore we do not believe in infant baptism.

10. We baptize by immersion for the remission of sins, according to Christ's commandment to be born again, when one has reached the age of accountability – able to know right and wrong – which begins at about age eight.

11. Rather than a heaven and a hell, we believe there will be three major gradations – kingdoms of glory – in the hereafter.

12. We believe that the ultimate goal for all mankind is exaltation – to live the life that God lives and to be in His presence.

13. We believe Satan is a real individual. In our pre-earthly existence, he was known as Lucifer, an advanced spirit who rebelled against God and became the embodiment of evil.

14. We believe Christ organized a church during His earthly ministry, that men changed it, and that the true church – doctrine, authority, practices, and organization – disappeared from the earth for over 1500 years.

15. We believe that God and Jesus Christ both appeared to 14-year-old Joseph Smith, Jr. in 1820, and called him to be the prophet through whom original Christianity would be re-established.

16. We claim to be the re-established original Christian church, founded on a base of prophets and apostles, as was the New Testament church.

17. We believe God gives continuous revelation to His prophets and apostles.

18. We believe the Bible. In English, we accept the King James Version. We also believe in additional scriptures such as the Book of Mormon. Neither book takes precedence because we believe both come from God.

19. The Book of Mormon is another testament – additional evidence – that Jesus Christ is the Son of God. It relates the history of a Christian people led by Christian prophets on the American continent from about 600 BC to 422 AD.

20. We believe that the priesthood – the power and authority to act in the name of God and Jesus Christ – was brought back and conferred upon Joseph Smith by heavenly messengers in 1829. These messengers were John the Baptist and Peter, James, and John.

21. We believe a man must be properly authorized to perform religious ordinances in the name of Jesus Christ. It is not enough to feel oneself called to this priesthood. A man must receive the priesthood from those who can trace their line of authority back to Jesus Christ.

22. We believe that there are those holding the priesthood who have the same sealing power that Christ gave to Peter – the power to bind or "seal" families together forever.

23. Polygamy was practiced in the early days of the church. It was not a church-wide practice, but was a commandment of God to specific individuals. In 1890, God directed that it cease. Since that time, it is no longer practiced and a member will be excommunicated if he does.

24. We celebrate the Sabbath on Sunday.

25. In our weekly worship services, the sacrament of the Lord's Supper, consisting of bread and water, is administered to members in remembrance of Christ's sacrifice and atonement.

26. We build temples so that special ordinances, such as marriage for eternity, can be administered in them.

27. In temples, we perform ordinances by proxy for those who died without knowing of Christ's true gospel. Those in the spirit world continue to be conscious, thinking individuals, and they can accept or reject this work done in their behalf.

28. The church is financed through tithing – 10% of one's income.

29. We subscribe to a health code in which we abstain from alcohol, tobacco, coffee, and tea.

30. We believe that Christ will return, usher in the Millennium, and be recognized by all people as the Messiah.

PART I

ANSWERS
ABOUT BELIEFS

CHAPTER 1

"Mormons Aren't Christians"

S ometimes it seems that the only way certain Christian groups will accept us Mormons at the table is if we're on the menu.

The reasons stem from disagreement over the physical characteristics of the resurrected Jesus Christ and the nature of the Godhead, topics we'll discuss in later chapters.

Mormons believe that anybody who worships Jesus Christ is a Christian, and that each individual deserves to be his own arbiter on the matter.

I don't think this definition is so complicated, but apparently for one of my former neighbors, it was. He was convinced that I couldn't possibly be a Christian "because you're a Mormon," as he so logically put it.

Sensing the fruitless journey I was about to embark on, I nonetheless asked him what it takes to be a Christian, and the conversation went something like this:

"You have to believe that Jesus Christ is the Son of God."

"I believe that with all my heart," I replied.

"You have to believe that Christ died for your sins on the cross, was buried in a tomb, and arose on the third day in triumph as a resurrected Being."

"Absolutely agreed. What else?"

"Well, you have to accept Jesus Christ as your Savior."

"I have done that, and I'm very grateful."

"You have to pray to the Father in Christ's name."

"Every morning and every night and three times a day in blessings on the food. What's next?"

Every definition he presented, I met. Roger that. Check, check, and check. Still not good enough.

It boiled down to one simple reason: I wasn't a Christian because I wasn't a member of *his* denomination.

This is the you-can't-belong-to-my-tree-house-club thinking we Mormons often face from some in the Christian community.

Where are those striped-shirt referees when you need them?

Old Testament Prophets Were Christians

My polling firm asked our sample of 1000 Americans when they believe Christianity began. Here are their perceptions:

Prior to Christ's birth	21%
When Christ was born	25
When He began His ministry	10
When He was crucified, resurrected	11
Since New Testament times	8

Only one in five thinks the answer lies any further back than Christ's birth.

So here is my question: If Christ is indeed the Son of God, which we affirm in the strongest of terms, does it make sense that God the Father would have given a different religion to our first parents, Adam and Eve, than Jesus Christ would teach when He was on the earth? Of course not. We reason from this that Christianity did not begin with the earthly birth of Jesus. The religion that Adam and Eve were taught by God was Christianity.

Then does that mean that every Old Testament prophet was a Christian? Yes, that is what we believe.

Mormons claim to be the re-established original Christian church

---

From the beginning, Adam and Eve taught their children Christianity – that the Son of God would one day come to the earth, teach His doctrines in person, and then atone for (that is, make forgivable) all the sins of mankind from the beginning to the end.

In time, the descendants of Adam rejected it, causing a falling away from true teachings, what we call an apostasy. Thus began a pattern: True Christianity was given to a prophet – Adam, Noah, Abraham, Moses, Isaiah, among others – followed by a falling away from those teachings. But in each era of time, each prophet knew of Christ,

Adam and Eve

Two out of three (68%) believe Adam and Eve were real people, while 28% believe they are fictitious characters.

Mormons maintain they are real.

knew Him to be the Son of God, and even knew what His name would be. That is why so many instructions given to people in Old Testament times were designed to focus their minds on the coming of the Messiah. In fact, we believe Jesus Christ is the Jehovah of the Old Testament and He, Himself, gave those instructions to those prophets.

All of which means Christianity has been periodically manifested throughout history, not just since the time of Christ.

The Reason for Our Name

So what does this have to do with Mormonism?

Look at the nine words – the understandable but often overlooked five and the funny four – of our formal name: The Church of Jesus Christ of Latter-day Saints.

The word *of*, signifying ownership, appears twice. First and foremost, it is The Church **of** Jesus Christ – that great Being we worship, the Son of God. It belongs to Him and He specifies the rules – the doctrine, organization, ordinances, commandments, and who is assigned to do what.

Second is the phrase "...**of** Latter-day Saints." The church also belongs to all of us today – that is, everyone and anyone who freely chooses to play by those rules. To them Christ gives authority to act in His name to bring others to an understanding of what He has done for us.

Are Mormons Christians?

By a two-to-one margin (58-28), Americans believe Mormons are Christians – 25% answer definitely yes to the question, while 33% are hesitant and say only probably so; 14% are definitely sure they aren't.

Uncertainty level (those who gave the wrong answer, are not sure, or don't know): 75%

Jesus Christ calls this secondary group of owners or adherents *saints*, a term condensed from the phrase "sanctified ones" and simply meaning *members*. (Catholics apply the term to someone who can be supplicated to intervene with Deity on their behalf. We do not subscribe to that definition and it is not applicable to our name.)

We are called The Church of Jesus Christ of *Latter-day Saints* to distinguish ourselves from the early Christians, who could be called members of The Church of Jesus Christ of *Former-day Saints*, and from the other manifestations of Christianity in history. Not that these names appeared on their T-shirts, but broadly speaking, there was a church, or religion, of Jesus Christ...

> ... of Adam's-day Saints,
>
> ... of Noah's-day Saints (there were only 8 of them),
>
> ... of Abraham's-day Saints,
>
> ... of Moses'-day Saints,
>
> ... of Isaiah's-day Saints, and of course
>
> ... of New Testament or Former-day Saints,

... each manifestation of Christianity being separated by a period of apostasy.

Our name understandably causes confusion when one wishes to use a shorthand reference. Here are our preferences:

- Our members are properly referred to as Mormons or as Latter-day Saints.

- Our church may be referred to by its full name or as the LDS Church.

- We prefer not to be called the Mormon Church, and we bristle a bit if we are referred to as the Church of the Latter-day Saints, a label that sounds like a formal title but leaves out the two most important words in our name.

The Mormon Claim

Such an apostasy, or general falling away, we believe also occurred after Christ's own mission. Christ presented His gospel and men changed it. They changed the ordinances, such as the form of baptism, they changed the organization, and they changed many of the doctrines. In fact, as Americans view Christianity today, only 36% believe things are the way Jesus Christ intended, while 57% believe something went wrong along the way.

The Claim

One in four (26%) have heard that Mormons claim to be the re-established original Christian church.

Once presented with that claim ...

5% say it definitely could be true

37% say it may or may not be true

51% say it definitely could not be true

Mormons claim that true Christianity has again been brought back. It is the same religion – the same teachings, same doctrines, same authority, same commandments, and, adjusting for unique circumstances of each era, the same organization – as existed in previous eras.

The last four words of our name tell the world our claim to be the final chapter of Christianity before Christ returns to the earth in glory. In nine simple words:

We claim to be the re-established original Christian church.

My question to my former neighbor and those who say Mormons aren't Christians: Why would we claim to be the **original** of something if we are not at least the **something**?

CHAPTER 2

"Mormons Don't Believe the Bible"

That is not true. We definitely believe the Bible.

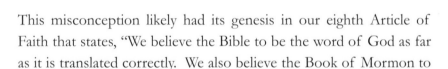

This misconception likely had its genesis in our eighth Article of Faith that states, "We believe the Bible to be the word of God as far as it is translated correctly. We also believe the Book of Mormon to be the word of God."

At the time our Articles of Faith were written in 1838, the average Christian on the farm or in the shop was not as aware of the mistakes and omissions that had crept into biblical manuscripts over the centuries – whether from careless scribes or theologians with agendas – as we are today.[2]   More people are now aware that no original manuscripts of any books in the Bible exist, so we do not know for sure how pure our present record is.

We Mormons have been belittled for the caveat – "as far as it is translated correctly" – in our statement of belief about the Bible, and that criticism has morphed into, ironically, an article of faith among our critics that Mormons therefore do not believe the Bible.

That qualifier today, however, looks astute, even prescient, as more Christians of every stripe and creed realize that mistranslations and errors in copying biblical manuscripts have occurred. As noted nearby, only 33% now believe the Bible to be the word of God, literally true word for word.

We believe the Bible as far as it is translated correctly, which has not always been the case

---

Our poll tested two versions of the claim that the Bible hasn't always been correctly translated. The stability of the attitude is apparent in that there are virtually no differences between the responses to these statements, each being asked of different halves of the sample:

Parts of the Bible have been changed since it was first written.

Strongly agree	37%
Somewhat agree	25
Somewhat disagree	9
Strongly disagree	22

Parts of the Bible have not been translated correctly.

Strongly agree	35%
Somewhat agree	28
Somewhat disagree	8
Strongly disagree	21

Those who take issue with what we submit is a reasonable caution, and by that infer that Mormons do not believe the Bible, would with the same logic have to say that the majority of Americans do not believe the Bible.

In short, we believe the word of God to be true as it came fresh and pure to the minds of inspired writers and through their quills to parchment. But we are not ready to endow that trait on all of the translators and scribes who subsequently handled the texts through the centuries.

Who Wrote the Bible?

Let's look at this canard about our not believing the Bible from another angle. We usually respond by pointing out that we are the Church of Jesus Christ, and that Christians obviously believe the Bible... that we study the Bible two out of every four years in our Sunday school classes... that we encourage Bible study in our homes... that our youth study the Bible in daily early-morning classes while they're in high school... that Mormons score higher on religious knowledge than other Christian religions,[3] and on and on.

Literal Interpretation

The Pew Forum on Religion and Public Life conducted a massive survey of the U.S. religious landscape in 2009. They gave respondents three choices regarding their view of the Bible and found about a third of the population in each category:

Word of God, literally true word for word	33%
Word of God, but not literally true word for word	30
Book written by men, not the word of God	28

But such illuminations don't seem to erase the misunderstanding in some quarters. There are still people (23%) who won't take "Yes we do" for an answer. Much as we declare that we believe the Bible,

Mormons and the Bible

Do Mormons believe the Bible?

Definitely Yes	**25%**
Probably Yes	35
Probably No	14
Definitely No	9

A high uncertainty level (75%), but a majority of Americans still grant that Mormons believe the Bible.

some think they know better what we believe than we do ourselves. So let me put it this way: We believe the Bible because we believe we are members of the same religion as those who wrote it. In a jocular way, we could even say that our "members" wrote it.

As explained in Chapter 1, we do not consider our membership to number only the 14 million or so who answer to the name Latter-day Saints, the adjectival phrase of Christ's church applied to His followers in our day. The Church of Jesus Christ – our broader church – includes members scattered throughout history, including every Old and New Testament prophet. It includes every person who wrote biblical text, such as:

- Moses, whose first five books of the Old Testament are saturated with references to and symbolism of the coming of the Messiah;

- Isaiah, who wrote eloquently about the coming of the Son of God, and whose works formed the libretto for *The Messiah*, Handel's famous oratorio;

- Daniel, Ezekiel, and Jeremiah, who chronicled Jehovah's dealings with the House of Israel;

- Zechariah, who prophesied when the Jews would recognize their Messiah in the last days;[4] and

- Matthew writing to the Jews, Mark writing to the Romans, Luke to the Greeks, John to those already converted to Christianity.

To such followers of Christ, we add the Christian prophets who wrote the Book of Mormon, and Joseph Smith and his successors as additional prophets in our era – all of them a special fraternity of prophets and other inspired writers who produce holy writ centered on Jesus Christ.

Mormons not only believe the Bible, we revere it and try our best to follow the God-given counsel found in its pages.

CHAPTER 3

"Mormons Don't Believe in the Trinity"

B elief in the Godhead is one thing; belief in the Trinity is a different matter.

We reject a doctrine that we maintain is based on a fraudulent insertion into the Bible.

As Christianity spread in the first and second centuries, new converts came from Jews and pagans alike. Both had trouble shedding old beliefs, especially in the worship of Deity. The Jews believed in one God; Greeks and Romans were accustomed to worshiping many.[5]

What to do? Who should Christians reach out to – the monotheistic or the polytheistic?

I don't know who it was – some say Tertullian, who was the first to use the Latin term *Trinitas* about 200 AD – but one of the pre-Nicene fathers came up with the idea of providing a three-in-one God: three gods for the polytheistic and one god for the monotheistic.

This "have it your way" (apologies to Burger King) description of the Godhead grew legs as bishops converged on Nicaea in 325 AD for a special council.

The Creedal Councils

Constantine, emperor of a fragmenting Roman empire, had had it with splintered and squabbling Christians. His predecessor, Diocletian, severely persecuted them in the first years of the 4th century, but Christianity came roaring back when Constantine proclaimed religious tolerance in 313 AD. He subsequently declared Christianity the universal church of the Holy Roman Empire (the word for universal being *catholic*) and ensconced it in his government administration. Though a sun-worshiper, he claimed his successes in battle flowed from Christ's protection, but did not convert to Christianity for almost 25 more years.

Mormons refuse to accept 4th-century creeds as the litmus test of Christianity

With renewed life, every sect of Christianity (estimates range in excess of 100) scrambled to carve out a favored position with the powerful, thus leading Constantine, who demanded stability and orthodoxy, to convene the famous Council of Nicaea to settle doctrine about the nature of God, His Son, and the Holy Ghost, and their relationship, once and for all.

The debate raged between the Trinitarians under Athanasius, who maintained that there were three co-equal Gods in one substance, and the anti-Trinitarians under Arius, who maintained that Christ was of a distinct substance from and subordinate to the Father. Constantine signaled his preference and the Arians were routed on a vote of 316 to 2. The three-in-one doctrine became the official position of the universal church of the Roman Empire.

The Council of Constantinople expanded upon the Nicene Creed a half-century later, and after a final chapter in the exhausting battle between Arians and Athanasians, the Catholic Church settled on the Athanasian Creed as the best explanation of the Trinity. It reads in part:

> We worship one God in Trinity, and Trinity in Unity, neither confounding the persons, nor dividing the substance. For there is one person of the Father, another of the Son, and another of the Holy Ghost. But the Godhead of the Father, Son and Holy Ghost, is all one; the glory equal, the majesty coeternal. Such as the Father is, such is the Son, and such is the Holy Ghost. The Father uncreate, the Son uncreate, and the Holy Ghost uncreate. The Father incomprehensible, the Son incomprehensible, and the Holy Ghost incomprehensible. And yet there are not three eternals, but one eternal. As also there are not three incomprehensibles, nor three uncreated; but one uncreated, and one incomprehensible. So likewise the Father is Almighty, the Son Almighty, and the Holy Ghost Almighty; and yet there are not three Almighties, but one Almighty. So the Father is God, the Son is God, and the Holy Ghost is God, and yet there are not three Gods but one God.

Whether one's worship leaned mono or poly, the Athanasian Creed provided support.

Its birth also evidences the influence of Greek philosophy on the early church. No more would truth come directly by revelation to apostles and prophets, but would be hammered out through argument and debate. Even today, 54% agree that religious truth can be discovered only through logic, human reasoning, and personal

MORMONS BELIEVE ... *WHAT?!*

experience.[6] The orators most adept in rhetorical skills would, therefore, have a disproportionate influence on what would be accepted as truth. An emperor's uplifted eyebrow was also not without impact.

We leave others to believe, worship, and adhere to whatever dogma they will. But we refuse to accept the creeds that came 300 years after the death and resurrection of Christ as the litmus test of Christianity. Even though 31% of America believes that tradition is just as good as scripture, we join with the 62% who do not.

We submit that tradition, no matter how comfortable and extensive, and rhetoric, however persuasive, can never substitute for scripture. Nor can either ever supplant direct and ongoing revelation to prophets as God's method for guiding His church.

The John Clause

The trouble was, scriptural support for the Trinitarian solution was thin. The Bible speaks often about the three members of the Godhead, but the word Trinity appears nowhere. In fact, the word *three* appears in only one New Testament verse alongside references to God the Father, and that's in the First Epistle of John (5:7), home of the famous Johanneum Comma. (The Comma here is not punctuation but a short clause, and goes to prove that if you have something simple to say, put it in Latin.) I'll de-Latinize the phrase and call it the John Clause.

Although the clause bears his name, John the Revelator, author of the epistle, did not write it.[7] Some zealous scribe along the way fraudulently inserted the phrase into this passage to change the meaning and provide support for the Trinity concept.[8] Here is how it reads with the John Clause highlighted:

For there are three that bear record **in heaven, the Father, the Word, and the Holy Ghost; and these three are one. And there are three that bear witness in earth**, the Spirit, and the water, and the blood: and these three agree in one.

The original verse only talked about three elements as symbols. The John Clause changed the meaning.

Trinitarians wrestle this scripture to support the three-in-one claim. They know, of course, about Christ's admonition to His apostles that they should be one as He and the Father are one, but such verses are not remotely supportive of the idea of three Gods of molecular unity because the apostles cannot possibly become twelve physical bodies in one.

As for the clause itself, one encyclopedia states that "nearly all recent translations have removed this clause, as it does not appear in older copies of the Epistle and it is not present in the passage as quoted by any of the early Church Fathers, who would have had plenty of reason to quote it in their Trinitarian debates (for example, with the Arians), had it existed then."[9]

Yet most Christians still subscribe to the creed, a paucity of scriptural support notwithstanding.

The John Clause is not related to Santa, but what a gift it was to the Trinitarians.

Mormons and the Trinity

America's belief about the Godhead or the Trinity depends on whether the focus is on *separateness* or *oneness*. As a sidebar shows, if the focus is on whether the members of the Godhead are separate or of one substance, historical tradition prevails and 66% accept the "one substance" theory.

If, however, the focus is on the meaning of *oneness*, then the picture is reversed and 58% agree that unity in purpose is more logical than unity in body.

Christ admonished His followers to be one as He and His Father are

The Trinity

Half of the Christians in the sample were asked: "Do you believe that God, Jesus Christ and the Holy Ghost are three separate Beings, or are they three Beings in one body or substance?"

Separate Beings	27%
Three in one body	66

The other half were asked: "The New Testament says that God, Jesus Christ, and the Holy Ghost are one. Do you believe that means they are one in purpose or one in body?"

One in purpose	58%
One in body	31

one. What could His disciples possibly gain if oneness meant a metaphysical combining of bodies, something that was not in their power to bring about in any case?

We Mormons believe, rather, that His commandment was a practical one for their benefit and for the advancement of His teachings – to be united in purpose and love and commitment. Most Americans grasp this when the choice is clearly presented.

When our critics say that Mormons do not believe in the Trinity, their goal is to paint us as non-Christians. They conveniently overlook our doctrine about the Godhead:

- Three Beings form the Godhead: God the Father, Jesus Christ the Son, and the Holy Ghost.

- They are separate Beings, unified in purpose but not in body, each having His roles.

- God the Father and Jesus Christ have glorified, tangible, physical bodies of flesh and bone (but not blood) – impervious to death, pain, and sickness – as will all of us upon our resurrection from the dead.

- The Holy Ghost is a Personage of spirit only.

That's it in a nutshell. No convoluted mental gymnastics to make a concept line up with scripture.

So if our critics say we are not historical Christians, we agree with them. We are, rather, New Testament Christians who do not believe in the Nicene Creed and the other man-made creeds that came along three centuries after Christ's ministry.

We believe in the Godhead, but not in the Trinity as defined.

CHAPTER 4

"Mormons Worship Joseph Smith"

We no more worship Joseph Smith than early Christians worshiped Peter.

We only worship God and Jesus Christ.

Indulge me in this chapter that Christianity may have gone astray over the centuries necessitating the re-establishment of the original Christian church. With that in mind, here is a short version of how we view history up to the early 1800s:

- Christ established a church during His earthly ministry. He gave the power to act in His name to Peter and the other apostles.

- Men persecuted those chosen leaders and eventually killed all but one of the apostles, leading to a weakening of leadership.

- Almost immediately after Christ's crucifixion and resurrection, men began to change His organization and teachings. In time…

  They altered the mode of baptism.
  They altered the teachings about the nature of the Godhead.
  They altered the teachings of repentance and forgiveness.

> They altered the understanding of the Fall of Adam.
> They eliminated the offices of prophets and apostles.
> They discontinued temple worship.
> They fell prey to Greek and Roman philosophies.
> They mixed ecclesiastical and secular authority.

- Christ, knowing all of this would happen, withdrew the authority to act in His name, His true church disappeared, and the world entered the Dark Ages of apostasy.

As has been foretold for centuries, the time will come when Jesus Christ will return to the earth in triumphal glory. But before that great day, there must be preparations. Here are the three preparatory steps as we understand them.

- Men's hearts would have to be turned toward learning and freedom, and the Bible would have to become available to all. We thank the reformers – Martin Luther, John Calvin, John Wycliffe, Ulrich Zwingli, Jan Hus, John Wesley, William Tyndale, et al. – for playing their forerunner roles, many of them dying as martyrs. We believe that they were guided by God.

- A nation would have to be founded where religious liberty would prevail. We thank Washington, Jefferson, Madison, Franklin, Adams, and so many others who brought this about. They, too, were inspired by God.

- The true church with its attendant authority to act in Christ's name would then have to be re-established, and a people prepared to receive Christ.

We Mormons believe that these preparations would not spontaneously happen. We believe it was imperative that God call a prophet to the task.

But who? What age? What background? What education?

The Search for a Prophet

None of the prophets in Old and New Testament times had an easy life. They were beaten up pretty badly – mocked, accused, hounded, and in many cases killed. A modern-day prophet would have to possess the same mettle.

If someone wanted only enough credibility to start a church, wouldn't one vision have been enough?

So, if it were up to you, where would you look? Perhaps intellectuals in a faculty lounge? Among the silver-spoon rich and famous, or the politically powerful?

Silly to even think such pockets of privilege might produce a prophet tough enough to carry out one of the most important missions in history.

No, you would search among the hardest of workers. You would select a leader to play the same role that Peter played in the original church – someone who put bread on the table by dint of hard work, but was also teachable and could become a leader of men.

Peter and his partners, two brothers named James and John, were small-business entrepreneurs. They owned boats, hired people, worked hard, worked smart, worked independently, and traded carefully. Rough and reeking of fish, they were not what people today would expect a prophet to look and smell like.

Peter was tough, willing, and impulsive. But he wasn't ready at the beginning of the Savior's three-year ministry to lead the church after Christ's departure. He had to be seasoned, brought along carefully, given trials such as his denying Christ three times that fateful night.[10] But the Savior knew Peter's heart and what he could become.

You would look for a young man with the qualities of Peter.

A Modern Prophet

Joseph Smith was poor, hard working, and teachable. When he was in his early teens, upstate New York was a hothouse of religious competition, each denomination claiming to have the truth. So intense were the religious revivals that the evangelizing movement became known as the Second Great Awakening, and western and central New York as the burned-over district, meaning there were no more unconverted souls, "fuel" as it were.[11]

Joseph attended as many revival meetings as occasion allowed, and listened carefully to the claims. If one denomination had the truth and the others didn't, it wasn't apparent to him. He later wrote that he often asked himself, "Who of all these parties are right; or, are they all wrong together? If any one of them be right, which is it, and how shall I know it?"[12]

An avid Bible reader, Joseph came across a passage in James one evening that said if anyone lacks wisdom, let him ask of God. Sounded reasonable, so one spring morning he went into a secluded grove of trees and prayed about which church he should join. This 14-year-old had no desire to start a church or be a prophet, only a wish to know which one was right.

He got his answer and a lot more.

We believe that God the Father and Jesus Christ appeared to Joseph Smith and told him to join none of them, and that he would be the means by which the original Christian church would be re-established.[13]

We Mormons try to be sensitive in explaining this event, but in last analysis it's what we believe, and that's what I promised to lay out for you.

Here are the reasons Jesus Christ told Joseph Smith to join none of the existing churches:

- Preachers of the day had a form of godliness but didn't really believe in God's power.
- They taught for doctrines the commandments of men.
- They paid lip service to God, but their hearts were far from Him.
- The professors of religion were all corrupt.
- Their creeds were an abomination.
- They were all wrong.

It was a tough and shocking message, no two ways about it. But note that it did not blame the individual members of the existing churches. It was directed at the preachers, the professors of religion, their hearts, their doctrines, and their false creeds.

I have also mused about it from this angle: If a teenager made up a story about a vision from God and Christ, hoping to become popular, wouldn't you think that he'd be a tad more diplomatic?[14]

But if Christ did indeed appear to Joseph, and

Joseph Smith

Do Mormons worship Joseph Smith?

Definitely Yes	11%
Probably Yes	18
Probably No	22
Definitely No	**14**
No Opinion	35

Uncertainty level: 86%

Christianity had indeed strayed from its original form and doctrine, is it not logical that Christ would deliver an explicit explanation of why His re-established church was going to be a different ride from the one that the leaders of other churches were operating?

And what a ride it was. Here are the events we believe actually happened in modern times:

1820: God the Father and His Son Jesus Christ appear to Joseph Smith. This is known as the First Vision.

1823: A heavenly messenger named Moroni begins a four-year series of visitations during which he instructs Joseph about an ancient record written by people who lived on the American continent from 600 BC to about 420 AD.

1828-29: Joseph Smith translates and publishes this record – the Book of Mormon, Another Testament of Jesus Christ – which includes an account of the Savior appearing to people on the American continent a few weeks after His resurrection.

1829: John the Baptist appears to Joseph and gives him the Aaronic Priesthood, holders of which have the authority to baptize.

1829: Peter, accompanied by James and John, appears to Joseph Smith and gives him the Melchizedek Priesthood, the same higher priesthood these three apostles held in their earthly ministry, and by which Joseph Smith was ordained an apostle. An ancient apostle brings the apostolic power to a new apostle.

1830: On April 6, The Church of Jesus Christ of Latter-day Saints is formally organized in upstate New York. It is established on a foundation of prophets and apostles, Jesus Christ being the cornerstone. Although not a full-blown organization when it was started with only six members, other offices – the same offices as in the New Testament church such as bishops, patriarchs, high priests, seventies, priests, teachers, deacons, etc. – were established as it grew.

1836: Moses, Elias, and Elijah appear to Joseph Smith and give him special authority to conduct all business related to preparations for the Second Coming of Christ. Joseph is given the same sealing power – the power to seal in earth and in heaven – that Christ gave to Peter.

1844: Joseph becomes a candidate for U.S. president to focus the public on the persecution Mormons were suffering. In June of that year, he dies in Carthage, Illinois, a martyr in a hail of mob bullets.

All in all, Joseph Smith claimed to have had personal visitations from God, Jesus Christ, Moroni, Adam, Noah, Abraham, Moses, Elias, Elijah, John the Baptist, Peter, James, and John – a veritable Who's Who of Religion. While the First Vision and the visits from Moroni were given to Joseph alone, at least one other person witnessed most of the other visions.[15]

Fairly tough to wrap your mind around at one telling, but that's what we believe. If Joseph had made it all up and wanted only enough credibility to start a religion, wouldn't one vision have been enough?

As it stands, there is no middle ground. Either all of these visitations happened or it is the biggest fairy tale since Goldilocks.

When our critics mistake our appreciation for Joseph Smith and his God-assigned work, and say we worship him, we reply that we no more worship Joseph Smith than New Testament Christians worshiped Peter. Neither man was divine. Both made mistakes. Joseph merely occupied the same leadership position in the re-established church that Peter held in the original church. Peter and Joseph — same apostleship, similar martyrs, kindred spirits.

Yes, the Bible warns us of false prophets. We believe that implies there must also be true prophets.

CHAPTER 5

"Mormons Add to the Bible Even Though God Said Not To"

If God held a televised news conference, would you watch it? If so, do you think you would learn something new?

Maybe there's more that God wants to tell us.

I find it puzzling that some people want a closed canon – as if the Bible is the be-all and end-all of what God (in Whom 88% of us believe) wants us to learn, and that by reading it one has finished school.

We Mormons make a simple claim: God still speaks to His children through a prophet because there is much more knowledge He wants to give to help us with life's test. Those of an opposite persuasion claim that God commanded that nothing be added to the Bible.

Let's take a closer look.

- The charge not to add anything to the Bible is extrapolated from a verse in the 22nd chapter of Revelation:

For I testify unto every man that heareth the words of the prophecy of this book, If any man shall add unto these things, God shall add unto him the plagues that are written in this book.[16]

Heavy stuff. The problem for those using this statement to assert that there shall be no further scripture is that "this book" refers to the book of Revelation, not to the Bible as a whole. The Bible as we know it was not compiled in its present sequence, with Revelation last, until centuries after John wrote that verse. Further, Revelation may have been written before John's own three epistles.[17]

- Today's Bible is not even the same collection of scriptural books it once was. In the Bible's own pages are references to other books that were once accepted as scripture but which have been lost: Jasher, Solomon, Wars of the Lord, Samuel, Gad, Nathan, Ahijah, Iddo, and the list goes on. If these lost books happened to turn up in an archaeological dig, under what stretched rationale could a don't-add-anything-to-the-Bible person refuse to accept them? The Bible is obviously not a once-and-final collection of all books that contains all the words the Lord gave to His people in ancient times.

- If one found out that the Apostle Paul had written another letter to the Corinthians besides the two we have in the Bible, would that other letter be scripture? Well, Paul actually *did* write a letter to the Corinthians before he wrote the one we call First Corinthians, as he reminds them in the fifth chapter of that book.[18] So if that letter and the lost books would be accepted as holy writ if found today, why not then other inspired writings?

A Comparison

The need to be open to further knowledge is well accepted. When has mankind ever exhausted any topic of knowledge? When have we ever been justified in ignoring new insights, new facts, new information in any form?

The way I view it, if I took a course of study from a professor, would I think at the end of the last class that I had learned everything he could teach me? If I read one book from an author, would I think I had exhausted all he could tell me?

Why should one Bible contain all that God wants to tell us and all we need to know?

Well, if we admit that we cannot drain all the knowledge available from one fallible person in one book or one class, why do we think one Bible contains all that God can or wants to tell us?

When we Mormons tell the world that there are additional scriptures, the standard answer we hear is that God may have more that He could say, but He has given us "all we need to know."

We submit that the differing interpretations of the Bible are *prima facie* evidence that, indeed, mankind does *not* have all it needs to know.

The Elitist Attitude

All people like to think they are knowledgeable and up on things. Some, however, get carried away with their accomplishments and not only feel they are above the intelligence of the huddled masses, but have all the knowledge they need. In such hubris lies a fall.

Consider a few of the dumber things that have been said by intelligent people about new knowledge:

- "This [atomic bomb project] is the biggest fool thing we have ever done. The bomb will never go off, and I speak as an expert in explosives." Admiral William Leahy to President Harry S. Truman, 1945.

- "Heavier-than-air flying machines are impossible." Lord Kelvin, president, Royal Society, 1895.

- "There is no reason anyone would want a computer in their home." Ken Olson, president, chairman and founder of Digital Equipment Corp., 1977.

- "Louis Pasteur's theory of germs is ridiculous fiction." Pierre Pachet, professor of physiology at Toulouse, 1872.

- "This 'telephone' has too many shortcomings to be seriously considered as a means of communication. The device is inherently of no value to us." Western Union internal memo, 1876.

This elitist attitude, smug in present knowledge and too lazy to be curious about the new, can trip us up as the above examples show, but is especially dangerous when it comes to things of Deity, such as assuming that God has nothing of further importance to tell us.

The News Conference

While many people are skeptical about the idea of additional scripture, this doesn't mean they would not be curious if God held a news conference.

We asked half of our national sample this question:

> If God held a televised news conference, would you watch it? *(If yes:)* And do you feel you would learn something new, or not?

> Would watch it and would learn something new   81%
> Would watch, but would not learn something new   5
> No, would not watch it   7

The other half of the sample heard the same question, but the follow-on choices were worded: "And do you feel you would learn something new, or that all He would say is already in the Bible?"

> Would watch it and would learn something new   68%
> Would watch, but it would already be in the Bible   14
> No, would not watch it   11

When the Bible is mentioned, some people feel cross-pressured and hesitate to say God would say something that is not in the Bible. But, more importantly, at least two out of three adults would watch expecting to learn something new. The underlying attitude is obvious: God can indeed tell us something we don't know. And I doubt any believer would label His message unimportant.

Therefore, I ask: Why can there not be equal curiosity in God's words if the mode of delivery is the printed page instead of an electronic medium?

The Book of Mormon: Another Testament of Jesus Christ

In light of these findings, let's look at what we believe is an additional collection of God's word to His children, the Book of Mormon.

It was written, as stated on its title page, "... to the convincing of the Jew and Gentile that Jesus is the Christ...."

Within that mission statement, the relevant question about the Book of Mormon is whether it can tell people something they don't know, give guidance, illuminate Christ's doctrines, solidify beliefs in Christ, and otherwise make them better. We think it can.

Is Revelation Possible?

In 2008, we asked:

Religious revelation is when God speaks to a person, such as Moses or Abraham, who then instructs people what God wants them to do. Do you believe that religious revelation stopped with the death of Christ's apostles, or that religious revelation is still possible today?

Stopped with the apostles	10%
Still possible today	83

In 2011, we asked two yes-no questions on the topic and found that ...

- 61% believe God still talks to prophets today, and
- 73% believe visions from heaven are possible today

Regardless of how the polling question is phrased, solid majorities believe in religious revelation, visions, and that God speaks to prophets.

And Joseph Smith was hammered for so asserting in 1820.

As indicated earlier, Joseph Smith was tutored by an angel named Moroni who, in his mortal time on earth, was a prophet who taught his people of the divinity of Jesus Christ. His father, Mormon, abridged a thousand-year record onto sheets of gold, the golden plates one hears about. In 1827, Joseph was entrusted with this ancient record and, we believe, through the power of God translated and published it to the world as the Book of Mormon.

Much has been written about this book. Some seek to dismiss it by picking at the admittedly miraculous circumstances of its appearance, the gold plates on which the text was engraved in a language called reformed Egyptian, the method of translation through the Old Testament instruments called a Urim and Thummim, and the improbability that a young man with only a few years of education could have produced it (which is like dismissing a baseball player's batting average by discussing what he was like growing up). Others write satirical musicals about it.[19]

We say that the only way to know whether the Book of Mormon might offer useful, new knowledge is to at least browse through it.

Allow me to quote a few of my favorite points of theology and philosophy found in its pages.

- **Knowledge of Christ:** We knew of Christ and had a hope of his glory many hundred years before his coming.

- **Faith:** Ye shall be called the children of Christ, for he hath spiritually begotten you; for your hearts are changed through faith on his name.

- **Salvation:** There shall be no other name given whereby salvation can come unto the children of men, only in and through the name of Christ, the Lord Omnipotent.

- **Natural man:** The natural man is an enemy of God and will be forever unless he yields to the enticings of the Holy Spirit and puts off the natural man through the atonement of Christ.

- **Cleanliness:** No unclean thing can inherit the kingdom of God.

- **Service:** When you are in the service of your fellow beings, you are only in the service of your God.

- **Voice of the people:** It is not common that the voice of the people desires anything that is contrary to that which is right; but it is common for the lesser part of the people to desire that which is not right; therefore you shall do your business by the voice of the people.

- **Learning:** To be learned is good if you hearken unto the counsels of God.

- **Riches:** Before ye seek for riches, seek ye for the kingdom of God. And after ye have obtained a hope in Christ ye shall obtain riches, if ye seek them; and ye will seek them to do good – to clothe the naked, feed the hungry, liberate the captive and administer relief to the sick.

- **Opposition:** It must needs be that there is an opposition in all things. If not, all things must be a compound in one.

- **Weakness:** I give unto men weakness that they may be humble; for if they humble themselves before me, and have faith in me, then will I make weak things become strong unto them.

- **Actions:** Wickedness never was happiness.

Three out of five Americans (61%) believe, as we do, that God still talks to prophets today. We hope they will look around to find where those words might be written.

CHAPTER 6

"Mormons Believe That Jesus and Satan Are Brothers"

S ounds blasphemous, doesn't it?

The fact is, we believe God is the Father of all of us, the Father of our spirits, and that we are all *spirit* siblings to one another as well as to Jesus, God's Firstborn Spirit, and a spirit named Lucifer, who became Satan.

To explain this, let's start with our belief that life is like a three-act play:

Act One: Our pre-earthly existence. We lived with God, the Father of our spirits. We grew, we learned, we progressed. Our lives did not begin at our earthly birth.

Act Two: Our earthly existence. Here we gain a body subject to pain and death, which fits in with the belief of 87% of all Americans that the human being consists of two parts, a body and a spirit or soul, the body being the house of the spirit. We are given agency to make decisions for ourselves. We experience trials and temptations in a world where things go wrong. From such we learn to recognize the good from the evil and are tested to see if we will obey God's commandments. To make it a valid test, our memory of Act One is erased.

Act Three: Life after death. When at death our spirit leaves our body, we will live in a spirit world until the day of resurrection when our spirits will be reunited with our bodies, glorified and incapable of sickness, pain, or death. We will then be judged and rewarded according to our actions on earth.

Now a few details.

The Role of Opposites

For centuries people have wrestled with a seeming conundrum. If God is the Creator of everything in the universe, does this mean He created evil?

We approach that question with a seemingly simple proposition: there must be opposition in all things. A few examples:

- Could anything be identified as sweet if its opposite, bitterness, did not exist?

- Would we understand hot if we did not know cold?

- Would we recognize energy if we didn't know fatigue?

- Would there be love if there were no hate?

If something does not have an opposite, it cannot exist. All things are defined not only by what they are, but what they are not.

So it is with good and evil. Good cannot exist without evil as its defining opposite. And evil exists because good has always existed. (The *Star Wars* series got it closer than most people may realize – there must be a good side and a dark side of existence.)

We are God's spirit children and lived with Him before we came to earth

Therefore, when people ask whether God created evil, we say that He did not. He will not be involved in anything that is evil. But He recognized that just as He is the embodiment of good, one of His spirit children might one day choose to become the embodiment of the opposite.

And that is exactly what happened.

There Was a War in Heaven

An essential attribute of our Father's plan for our life on earth is our agency – the power to choose for ourselves whether we will follow good or evil – so that we progress by our own experience. Because of this God-given free will, we will make both good and bad decisions. We will make mistakes.

Therefore, the Father's plan, presented in Act One, required that one of God's spirit children be sent as the Son of God to live a perfect life and atone for the sins that mankind was sure to commit in an imperfect setting. Without such a Redeemer, we would remain separated from God forever.

Jesus Christ, the Firstborn and foremost of all of God's spirit children, volunteered to carry out the Father's will. He did not have to do it. God would not have forced Him. But He willingly chose to leave the glories of His home above and come to earth under primitive conditions to teach, show us the way to return to God's presence, and perform an atoning sacrifice for our benefit.

We are told in the Old Testament that we shouted for joy[20] at this chance to progress and become perfected through trials and tribulations, and, through sincere repentance for our mistakes and the mercy of the atonement of Jesus Christ, return to live with God for eternity.

That is, most of us shouted for joy. Others did not want to chance failing the test, and hesitated. They wanted guarantees that they would return.

Satan

Five out of eight (63%) believe Satan is a real person, while 32% believe he is a fictitious character. Among Christians, 76% believe he is real and 19% do not.

An earlier study (Barna, 1997) found that 62% believe Satan is not a living being, but rather a symbol of evil; 30% disagreed.[21]

One very intelligent spirit by the name of Lucifer saw an opportunity in that hesitation to marshal opposition to God's plan and to gain power. He, too, volunteered to become God's earthly son, but with a twist.

His idea was to deny people agency and become their agent instead, acting, supposedly, in their behalf to make sure all would return and none would be lost. He would do this by separating consequences from actions – that whatever people did would not be deemed a sin, and therefore they, being sinless, could return to their heavenly home.

For this great deed he wanted more than "Atta boy, Luce" adulations from those who chose to follow him. He wanted the glory and power of the Father – to reign in His stead.

Of course, it could never be. True progress can only occur when we take responsibility for our actions and learn from both our successes and our mistakes, the purpose of our coming to earth. So it was no surprise that the Father chose to send Jesus Christ, His Firstborn Son in heaven, to be His Only Begotten Son on earth.

Then the fireworks began. Not with the tools of war as we know them today, but with the most persuasive arguments that could be arrayed on both sides. We do not know how long it lasted, but when that phase of the battle between good and evil was over, one third of God's children chose to follow Lucifer.[22] The promise (hollow, as it turned out) of a return ticket without effort was too enticing.

In rebelling against the will of the Father, Lucifer, once privileged to sit in leadership circles, willfully chose to wrap himself in every evil characteristic that is necessarily co-existent with and in opposition to every good and worthy trait.[23]

He became the embodiment of evil, just as the Father and Jesus Christ are the embodiment of good. He became Satan, and with his followers was cast out upon the earth where they continue their evil designs, but without bodies.

And the heavens wept.

Jesus and Satan

Check our logic. When we refer to God as our Heavenly Father, as almost every denomination does, what is He the Father of? Obviously, He is the Father of our spirits, that part of us that is housed within our earthly body and gives us life. Note further that the two who volunteered to come to the earth and be the Redeemer were also spirit children of our Heavenly Father.

That being the case, it necessarily follows that every person is a *spirit* brother or sister to every other person who has ever lived or ever will live on the earth. When our critics parade in front of our temples with placards that say, "Jesus and Satan are not brothers!", they either misunderstand our teachings or intentionally seek to deceive by mis-characterizing them.

So not only is Jesus a spirit brother to Satan, but Moses is a spirit brother to Hitler, Abraham to Stalin, Noah to Genghis Khan. And so on. How could it be otherwise if we're all children of God?

In fact, one could say that the relationship between Jesus and Lucifer is the mother of all sibling rivalries.

About That Pre-Earthly Existence

To my knowledge, Mormons are the only ones prominently teaching about this pre-earth life. But there are hints in prose and practice that earth life is indeed Act Two of a three-act play.

You will find references to this pre-earthly existence in both the Old and New Testaments of the Bible.[24] From the Greek philosophers, we have Plato and Aristotle who danced around this concept with their ideas of *innatism* – pre-existing knowledge. And it's also found in early Christian writings

Before and After

Only 28% believe, as Mormons do, that we lived with God before coming to the earth; 61% believe life begins at birth. (2008)

Four out of five (78%) believe we live after death, while 17% say this life is all there is.

such as Origen of Alexandria who wrote about "the fabulous pre-existence of souls."[25]

Even poets reference that our existence pre-dates our conception. Consider the words of William Wordsworth from his *Intimations of Immortality*:[26]

> Our birth is but a sleep and a forgetting:
> The Soul that rises with us, our life's Star,
> Hath had elsewhere its setting,
> And cometh from afar:
> Not in entire forgetfulness,
> And not in utter nakedness,
> But trailing clouds of glory do we come
> From God, who is our home:
> Heaven lies about us in our infancy!

Go to any funeral today and chances are high that the mourners, if not the pastor himself, will use the phrase, "God called him home." Which leads to the question, "How can a place be called our home if we have never lived there?" How can we *return* to a place we have never been?

And then there are common sense observations. Did accomplished people develop their great talents from genes and environment alone, and in only a few short years?

- Was Mozart playing the piano at age three and composing at age five because of something in Salzburg's water?

- Did Leonardo da Vinci pick up his diverse talents from his quite common parents and the happenstance vibes of a 15th-century Italian countryside?

- Analyzing Thomas Jefferson's works, could we conclude that just anyone who happened to have been planted in Virginia for 33 years might have written the Declaration of Independence?

- Do we chalk up the mental acuity of a Kim Ung-yong, the record IQ holder who began studying physics at a university at age three, to simple six-sigma statistics – that somebody has to occupy that tail end of the bell curve for brilliance?

No. Logic cries out that there is more to us than we could possibly have acquired from gene pools and the environments of just our earthly upbringing. We were mature spirit children of heavenly parents before we came here.

We brought *us* with us.

CHAPTER 7

"Mormons Are a Cult"

When that word enters the room, civil Christian debate disappears.

Pie a la mode.

As one observer explained why people use the term: "Because it's a neat, shorthand and rather lazy way of putting a whole group into a box." [27]

Or it could be intentional polemics. Sun Tzu, a famous Chinese general who lived 500 years before Christ, advised heaping scorn and ridicule on an enemy's cherished traditions and institutions as a tactic to undermine the strength of an opponent. [28]

Today, similar denigration is recognizable in the use of the trendy label "cult" – a harsh, cold, four-letter word used to summarily dismiss religious competitors and avoid civil discourse. If a group is a cult, [29] as 26% actually believe about Mormons, then obviously an open-minded investigation of such inferiors is out of the question.

What Exactly Is A Cult?

Dictionary definitions of a cult have these elements in common:

- Relatively small group
- Excessive devotion to a person or idea
- Unethical techniques
- Control by threats and isolation
- Powerful group pressures
- Fear of consequences of leaving
- Abnormal dependency on the group
- Strange beliefs

To someone who knows Mormonism, these descriptions don't match up with our characteristics, but let's consider them one by one.

- **Small?** We have 14 million members in 132 countries. In America, there are more Mormons than there are Presbyterians or Jews.[30]

  The average American thinks that most Mormons live in Utah, but over half of all Mormons are not residents of the United States, and only 14% live in Utah, a percentage that is decreasing. For some name-callers, however, size doesn't matter: they even label Catholics a cult.

- **Excessive devotion?** We are devoted to the Savior, but in appropriate measure we think He would approve of.

- **Unethical techniques?** Ask the critics to name one.

- **Control by isolation?** Even if we wanted to, this would be impossible with 14 million members in 28,000 congregations throughout the world.

- **Control by threats?** Again, evidence? Our missionaries may be exuberant, but we do not threaten.

- **Dependency on the group?** Our goal is just the opposite. We want our members to be self-reliant and independent so they in turn can help others.

- **Powerful group pressure?** Only if that's the way our critics prefer to define love.

Perceptions

To the best of your understanding, about what percentage of Mormons live in Utah?

80% or more	13%
60% up to 80%	19
40% up to 60%	20
20% up to 40%	13
Less than 20%	9

The correct answer: 14%. Over half of all Mormons live outside the United States.

- **Strange?** There they've got us. We plead guilty to all the strange things that were done by Christians in New Testament times that were lost during the great falling away in the aptly named Dark Ages, among them temple worship, vicarious baptism for the dead, prophets and apostles, unpaid clergy, and continual revelation from God to guide His church.

Let others call us a cult if they feel such tactics will, more effectively than doctrine, attract followers. When Mormons hear that word spit at us, we can only wonder whether our accusers are all that confident in their own positions and legitimacy.

Ridicule Comes With the Territory

Calling us a cult today cannot be the first time in history that a religion has been ridiculed with that word or an equivalent pejorative.

Cult?

Are Mormons a cult?

Definitely Yes	11%
Probably Yes	15
Probably No	27
Definitely No	**36**

Uncertainty level: 64%

If Adam and Eve had had contemporary critics, our first parents surely would have been mocked as members of a nudist cult. And can you imagine the fun mockers must have had when Noah built a boat and gathered animals?

The Savior Himself did not escape it. He was mocked, scourged, spit upon, and put to death by the most cruel method devised by man because He dared to form what the elite, powerful, and supposedly wise of His day undoubtedly considered a cult.

Not every person who is smeared with ridicule is a prophet of God, but every prophet of God has been and will be smeared.

Real Cults Don't Laugh at Themselves

There's no law that says a cult can't have a sense of humor, but honestly, have you ever heard of one that did? Under controlling conditions and a leader claiming to be infallible and beyond criticism, there's no room in cult thinking for levity pointed at that leader or themselves. It would presage a loss of control.

As one thinks of such groups as the Jonestown bunch or the Waco Branch Davidians, it is hard to imagine in such groups the gentle, self-deprecating humor that is abundantly found in Mormondom.

We are respectful and reverent toward sacred things, but it's open season on our own culture. A few of my favorites:

- Why do Mormon women stop having babies at 35? Because 36 is just too many.

- What do you get when you cross a kleptomaniac and a Mormon? A year's supply of stolen food.

Cults do not exhibit the gentle, self-deprecating humor abundantly found among Mormons

---

- Who is the pushiest person in the world? A Mormon missionary with an Amway distributorship on the side.

- The last thing Satan wants is for Mormons to go to hell. With our irrigation expertise we'd ruin the place for him.

- By the way, heard about Jewish mothers? Let me tell you about Mormon fathers.

And that doesn't touch on our inside jokes, many of which deal with food – Cheerios, green Jell-o, funeral potatoes – which is understandable if you're not allowed to get a kick from coffee, tobacco, or booze.

Mormons a cult? Don't make me laugh.

CHAPTER 8

"Mormons Worship a Different Jesus"

The obvious intent of a few ministers and preachers here is to sow confusion about Mormon Christianity to discourage others from checking it out.

Considering the finances involved, I can't be too harsh on them for throwing such pies. After all, we are taking 800 parishioners from their ranks every day and constructing a new church building somewhere in the world every 16 hours to accommodate them.

Different religions will always have differing interpretations of scriptures. That's not a surprise. What is sad is when civil discussion about this topic fades and one group accuses another of worshiping a different person altogether – injecting a whiff of idol worship or chasing after strange gods.

The pro-LDS Foundation for Apologetic Information & Research (FAIR) explained it this way:

Latter-day Saints have no quarrel with the idea that some of their beliefs about Jesus may differ from those of other Christians. If there were no differences in belief at all, it would make little sense to have the hundreds of Christian denominations which exist.

But it is insulting and unfair to insist that the LDS do not worship the "same" Jesus as other Christians. By analogy, a Protestant might consider Martin Luther an inspired instrument in the hands of God to reform the wayward Christian Church. A Catholic might rather consider Luther to be a wayward priest who was gravely mistaken. Clearly, the opinions about Luther may differ, but it would be absurd to insist that Catholics and Lutherans are each talking about a *different* Luther.[31]

A more accurate way to criticize us would state that Mormons have a different understanding of the Savior's physical properties and the doctrine of the Godhead.

We'd buy that.

The Creeds Again

Theologians in other religions pounce on two of our beliefs as justification for saying we worship a different Jesus.

- We believe in a physical resurrection. Birth is the coming together of a spirit into a mortal body; death is the separation of the two; and resurrection is the recombining of spirit and body.

- As explained in Chapter 3, we do not subscribe to the three-substances-in-one theory of the Nicene Creed. We say, rather, that the three Personages in the Godhead are one in *purpose*, not one in substance. Jesus Christ is a distinct and separate Member of a three-person Godhead.

In our survey, 21% of all Americans agree with our concept of a physical resurrection, but 47% believe we will be resurrected as spirits only. The idea of a spiritual resurrection is puzzling to Mormons. Resurrection, as we understand it, means to rise again or to be reinstated. If the spirit continues to live after death while the body is in the grave, what is it that rises again, or is reinstated, in a spirit resurrection?

God, Jesus Christ, and the Holy Ghost are one in purpose, not one in substance

As we see things, the physical nature of the resurrected Christ is hard to miss. His spirit left His body on the cross and returned to take it up again from the tomb on that famous Sunday morning. He subsequently appeared to many and they felt His tangible body. Thomas, he of doubting fame, was told to put his finger into the print of the nails and thrust his hand into His side. Jesus Christ appeared on another occasion and told His disciples to handle His hands and feet "for a spirit hath not flesh and bones, as ye see me have," and then ate fish and honey with them.[32] Hardly the doings of a disembodied spirit.

Those who accept these events, but argue that Christ subsequently disposed of His resurrected body upon ascending into heaven, have difficulty finding evidence for their speculation.

As for our claim that the three members of the Godhead are separate Beings unified in purpose, consider a few of many pieces of the logical evidence available to any Bible-believing Christian:[33]

- Who spoke from heaven when Jesus was in the river Jordan being baptized?

- Did Christ address His pleas to Himself when He was in the Garden of Gethsemane?

- Did He commend His spirit into His own hands when He gave up the ghost on the cross?

- Was He seen by Stephen the martyr standing on His own right hand?

Resurrection

"Do you believe that there is life after death? *(If yes)*: Do you believe that we will be resurrected with tangible bodies or that we will live as spirits?

	All Americans	All Christians
Life after death / tangible bodies	21%	25%
Life after death / spirits	47	51
Life after death / don't know	10	11
No life after death	18	10
No opinion	5	3

Hard to believe that one in ten Christians rejects a central tenet of Christianity.

All Christians believe that God the Father is a God of both justice and mercy. But for justice to be served and mercy extended required a *separate* perfect Person, His Son, to be the Redeemer and pay the price of sin and mistakes for every person who will ever live on the earth. This also, we believe, points to a multiple-person Godhead – distinct and separate from one another, each with His special mission.

As it is, other Christian faiths speculate that Jesus Christ was reabsorbed into a molecular Trinity after His earthly ministry, while we believe there is ample evidence that the three Beings in the Godhead were and are corporeally separate, while unified in purpose.

Our Straightforward Declaration

Here is what we believe about Jesus Christ:[34]

- There is only one Messiah, one Savior, one Only Begotten Son – Jesus Christ.

- God has caused worlds without number to be created. This earth is not the only peopled planet.

- Jesus Christ is the Jehovah of the Old Testament. He created these worlds under the direction of God the Father.

- Christ agreed in the pre-earthly life to obey God's will and become our Redeemer.

- Christ came to this earth because there would be such great wickedness that people would crucify their own God.

- His birth, mission, and death were prophesied by Old Testament prophets, and He fulfilled the law of Moses.

- Jesus was without sin and, having led a perfect life, was the only One who could pay for the sins of all humanity.

- After His crucifixion and three days in the tomb, Christ overcame death and was resurrected as a glorious and perfect physical Being, thus providing for the resurrection of every person who will ever live on earth.

Horrible and Humiliating

Jesus Christ loved us so much that He was willing to endure the full weight of our sins and pay the most horrible and humiliating price to save us. Crucifixion is the most agonizing form of execution, and the loincloth in Renaissance art depicting the event did not exist.

- Jesus Christ, the Messiah, will return to usher in the Millennium.

- There is only one Atonement and one Redeemer.

- What Christ accomplished for all of mankind is the single most important event in history.

By definition, every Christian worships only one Jesus Christ. Intimating that there are two is demeaning of the Savior and does not belong in fair debate.

We worship Jesus Christ as the Messiah, the Mediator, and our Master.

We understand Him enough to know that agreements have two sides.

We trust Him enough to accept His conditions.

We love Him enough to do our best to obey Him.

CHAPTER 9

"Mormons Believe They Are the Only True Church"

Yes, we have used that phrase. But a more accurate statement is that we claim to be the only *authorized* church.

Debate over which church is true animated Americans in the early years of our nation, with great traveling revivals recruiting the unbaptized to one denomination or another – mass marketing 1800s-style. People understood that the phrase "true church" meant the religion that could lead them to heaven – it implied necessary authority.

The assumption that some church has to be the true one has faded. Today, 65% believe that many religions can be true (up six points since our 2008 survey), while only 25% believe there can be but one true religion. Most Christians do not place their own church on that pedestal. Only 16% of Catholics, long a bastion of belief in one true church, believe there is but one true church and 76% now subscribe to the many-true-religions position. Among Baptists, it's 28-64, and among evangelical Christians it's 43-51.

Eternal Life

According to the U.S. Religious Landscape Survey conducted by the Pew Forum on Religion & Public Life, 70% of Americans believe that many religions can lead to eternal life, and only 24% say that theirs is the one, true faith leading to eternal life.

Only two religions have a majority of their members claiming the latter: Jehovah's Witnesses at 80% and Mormons at 57%.

Perceptions of religious history have also been influenced by this multiplicity trend. We asked Christians in our sample, "When Jesus Christ and His apostles organized the Christian church in New Testament times, was it the only true religion on the earth, or not?" Only 42% said it was. And this in spite of what virtually all Christian churches teach today – that Jesus said that He is the way, the truth, and the life, and that no man comes to the Father but through Him.[35]

A further indicator of complex perceptions on this issue of a true church arose when we asked those who earlier had said that there are many true religions, "Do you feel that Mormons could or could not be one of those true religions?"

Tabulating across the whole sample, we find:

There is only one true religion	25%
Many true religions and Mormons could be one of them	50
Many true religions and Mormons are not one of them	10

Then, just for fun, I checked how those with an unfavorable impression of Mormons answered the question: 38% of them said Mormons could be one of the true religions.

So … a plurality of Christians do not believe that Christ established the only true religion, half of all Americans believe Mormons could be one of many true religions, and a sizeable chunk of people holding an unfavorable impression of Mormons nonetheless grants that the LDS Church may be among them.

My head hurts.

Our View of Other Churches

The phrase "true church" today leaves the impression that there is one church that has all truths and the rest do not.

Mormons do not believe that. We believe there are truths to be found in many religions, and that our fellow religionists do much good and preach many doctrines that are true. We seek to build on those truths with our invitation to the world: Bring the truths that you have and see if we can add to them.

The job of the authorized church is to help everyone get into heaven

---

The more appropriate question is not which church has truths, but which church has authority to act in the name of God and Jesus Christ. A church could teach impeccable doctrine, say, about baptism, but that would not in itself mean that the baptisms it performs are valid in God's eyes.

We understand that many will disagree with us when we claim that The Church of Jesus Christ of Latter-day Saints is the only authorized church on earth. We do not, however, state it out of arrogance or any need to feel superior. It is simply a natural consequence of believing that Joseph Smith had the vision he claimed.

Look at it this way. Why would God appear in a vision and tell the recipient to form a religion if there are many true religions already on the earth? Why would He add one more in a line of many?

So when one understands that we *really do* believe this vision happened, our claim should not be a surprise. Our puzzlement is why more churches don't claim to be the true or authorized church and offer their explanations for discussion – brand differentiation, if for no other reason. After all, Christ did not believe there were other true religions; He didn't submit a "Can't we all get along?" proposal to the Pharisees and Sadducees. And I am sure He would not do it differently today.

Here's our reasoning. Christ and His apostles organized the Christian church in New Testament times. If Christ's church was the only true church then (although only one in four Christians believe it), why would not His re-established church be the only authorized church now? The only point open to debate is whether or not He has re-established it. We believe He has; others believe He has not.[17]

Making a claim to have the true authority may not be unusual; but given the story we tell, *not* making the claim would be.

Doctrine and Permission

With that as background, we believe the church Christ founded did two things: it taught people correct doctrine, and with authentic authority performed ordinances necessary to get them into heaven, such as baptism. The first requires a correct understanding and the second requires permission.

Doctrine. Many claim they receive correct doctrine from the Bible. While the Bible indeed contains correct doctrine, its passages have been interpreted so differently by various denominations that an appeal to the Bible has rarely settled disputes. Thus, the differences in Christendom today are numerous – the mode of baptism, the nature of God, the purpose of life, church organization, responsibilities, repentance, the hereafter, good versus evil, rites and ordinances, the commandments, and on and on. It is one interpretation against another. True interpretation of the Bible can only come through direct revelations from God.

Permission. In the same vein, the Bible cannot be the source of permission to perform the ordinances that will be recognized in heaven. If it were, then anyone, with whatever cockamamie ideas he may drag along, would have just as much claim to officiate in behalf of Jesus Christ as anyone else who reads it. God's house would become a house of confusion, something He has said it is not.[36]

The standard response to the last point is that (1) permission really isn't needed, or if it is needed, that (2) people can pursue the ministry if they "feel themselves called" to the work. The survey found that by a slight 48-44 margin, Americans believe that no special ordination is necessary to become a minister as long as one feels called to the ministry.

We believe that is a recipe for chaos. (Maybe I'll feel myself called to drive my neighbor's car; I'm sure he wouldn't mind.)

Authority Counts

Consider this analogy. I could read up on legal procedures and nail down the jargon, but if I have not been given standing by a court – if I am not authorized to practice as an attorney – brilliant arguments, smashing orations, impeccable logic avail nothing.

Doctrinal sermons may be dazzling, but without authority given by God, they cannot, in end analysis, substitute for authority.

We claim to have both correct doctrine and permission. Ongoing revelation from God keeps the doctrine pure, and authority, as noted earlier, came directly from the same people who held that permission in the days of Christ's earthly ministry.

That said, the LDS Church does not feel it has a corner on truth. It does maintain, however, that it has a corner on the authority to perform valid ordinances in the name of Jesus Christ.

And the job of the authorized church is to help everyone get into heaven.

CHAPTER 10

"Mormons Believe They Can Work Their Way Into Heaven"

No, we do not believe we can work our way into heaven. Nor, at the other end of the scale, do we believe in E-Z Pass grace.

For centuries, Christians have fiercely debated what it means to be saved. The only commonly accepted result is that there is no commonly accepted definition. No surprise that denominations talk past each other.

Maximizing gain while minimizing effort has driven mankind since fig trees were clothing stores, and no one likes his business model challenged. It is no different when the goal is to be saved and go to heaven.

It's all about return on investment.

Six Meanings of "Being Saved"

The best analysis I have read of what it means to be saved comes from Dallin H. Oaks, former Utah Supreme Court justice, former president of Brigham Young University, and now an apostle in our church. Elder Oaks suggests these definitions, which I quote or paraphrase as follows:[37]

	Meaning	Comment
1	Saved from the permanence of death through the resurrection of Jesus Christ.	A free gift to everyone who has been or will be born.
2	Saved from our sins and the consequences of sins.	Through the atonement of Christ, we can be saved by obeying His commandments.
3	Saved in the sense of being "born again."	We are born again when we are baptized and take upon ourselves the name of Christ.
4	Saved from the darkness of ignorance.	As we learn the teachings of Jesus Christ, we come out of darkness and into light.
5	Saved in the sense of being delivered from a final spiritual death.	All but a very few[38] are assured of a kingdom of glory in the world to come.
6	Saved in the sense of exaltation or eternal life.	God desires us to become perfect that we may become as He and Christ are.

The atonement of Christ makes all of these aspects of salvation possible.

The most confusion arises when one person refers to the second meaning – being saved from our sins – while the listener visualizes the first or the third.

We believe that it is not enough alone to confess that Jesus Christ is our personal Savior, and go merrily on our way. To believe in a once-and-for-all declaration and a that's-that attitude is like taking a bath once and never touching soap again. It takes constant effort to resist the temptations of the world.

Does that sound unreasonable? Yet it is from this simple notion – that we are required to keep the Lord's commandments – that our critics manufacture the misconception that we believe we can work our way into heaven.

The full power of Christ's atonement requires us to do our part

They say Mormons place too much emphasis on works. We say their interpretation of grace minimizes the responsibility we all have to repent and keep God's commandments, and we ask, "If confessing Christ is sufficient, why bother to go to church?"

They respond that a sincere confessor will do good works out of love for Christ, not fear of punishment. We agree, but for those who don't, is it possible for a person to fall from grace, to not be saved even though he has confessed Christ?

And the interesting debate will continue.

I will grant part of their argument. We are an achievement-oriented religion. We encourage our members to serve others, pay an honest tithing, refrain from harmful substances, keep sexual relations within the bounds of marriage, and obey the other commandments.

We are not passive; our religion is a 24/7 way of life.

The All-Encompassing Atonement of Jesus Christ

Being saved by any definition requires the grace of Jesus Christ.

A professor friend of mine tells of dining with a minister of another religion and his wife. When the conversation focused on the fate of those who were born before Christ, the minister's wife said, in essence, they were out of luck. We hope that attitude is not prevalent among those not of our faith, but it serves as a contrast to what we believe – that Christ's sacrifice is not solely for those fortunate to be born after His resurrection. I found a deeper appreciation for Christ's atoning grace when Tad R. Callister pointed out its four dimensions.[39]

Backward. Just as Christianity did not begin in 30 AD, the blessings of the atonement did not wait for Christ's death on the cross. They came into effect the moment Christ accepted the assignment from the Father in our pre-earthly existence. Just as a person can enjoy a meal at a restaurant before paying for it, so too could those who were born before Christ's ministry enjoy the power of His atonement before He paid the actual price – His promise was good.

Forward. The efficacy of the atonement extends forward into eternity for all who will ever enter mortality, our life on earth.

Height. If Christ created worlds without number under the Father's direction, as we indeed believe, it is only reasonable that His sacrifice would be valid for those on each of them. The actual crucifixion could only take place on one earth, but the atonement's power reaches into every corner of God's creations.

Depth. Christ came to the earth to experience first-hand every temptation that could be thrown at Him, to comprehend them, but not succumb to them, so He would know how to give us compassion and love. There would be no temptation or sin that the Savior would not understand. Because of His perfect life, no sin, mistake, problem, or emotional burden would fall outside the effectiveness of His atonement.

All Christians recognize and appreciate what Christ did for us during His earthly ministry. But the knowledge of what Christ did before He came to the earth – as I explained in Chapter 6 – is an additional reason why we Mormons are all the more grateful for His life and mission.

Christ said explicitly that if we love Him, we must keep His commandments. That means effort.[40] We do not say that we love Christ more than other Christians do because we recognize this need to keep His commandments and expend effort doing so. Not at all.

But neither do we love Him less.

Grace

We Mormons would place ourselves at the mid-point of the scale noted at the beginning of this chapter. We cannot work our way into heaven, but we are expected to put in the effort to keep the Lord's commandments. The sum of our belief is this thought from the Book of Mormon:

> It is by the grace of Christ that we are saved *after all we can do.* (Emphasis added.)

Grace, as we understand it, is the love, mercy, and enabling power of the atonement that allows our sins to be forgiven and provides the opportunity to live in God's presence forever.

In 2008, my polling firm asked Christians in our randomly chosen sample which of two definitions of grace they believed:

> People are saved by the grace of Christ if   57%
> they will only recognize Him as their Savior
>
> People are saved by the grace of Christ only   37
> after they do their best to live His commandments

In other words, a majority of Americans believe that recognizing Jesus Christ as their Savior is sufficient for one to be saved, nothing further needed. Three out of eight, on the other hand, lean toward the LDS concept of grace – not a bad showing for the doctrine considering that Mormons constitute barely 2% of the U.S. population.

Mormons believe that unconditional grace applies only to the first type of salvation – that all of us will be resurrected as a free gift. The grace of Christ is necessary for all others as well, but each is conditioned upon effort, faith, and obedience on our part.

Another look at the six types of being saved may clarify what we believe is expected of us.

Number 1: Saved from death. Every person who occupies an earthly body will be resurrected and thus, in that sense, saved. Such a saving, however, does not necessarily place one in heaven.

Number 2: Saved from sins. This salvation comes from working with the Savior to repent of our sins and follow His counsel. We will be judged according to our works and deeds, or lack thereof, and where our heart was as we did them. Actions must have consequences.

Mormons do not believe in just a heaven for the good and a hell for the bad, an either-or, saved-or-not-saved, two-part hereafter. Rather, we believe there are three kingdoms of glory in the

Works and Grace

The word *works*, as in working one's way into heaven, has acquired a negative flavor, whereas deeds and actions not as much.

When phrased "God will judge us by what we do on earth," agreement is 79%. But describe the concept by using words such as *works*, *reward* and *punish* – "God will reward or punish us depending on our works" – and agreement drops to 51%.

Same concept, different words.

We do not believe that all one needs is willpower and discipline, and the pearly gates swing open. But we do believe that deeds are part of the equation and that actions must have consequences.

hereafter – celestial (where God dwells), terrestrial, and telestial[41] – even the lowest of which surpasses this world in joy and happiness. (This concept is also found in Paul's writings.)[42]

Number 3: Saved by being born again. When we are born again through baptism, we promise Christ that we will take His name upon us – be called a Christian – and keep His commandments. We are to have faith in Him and repent of our sins – real hope and change. As we do our best to change our ways, we receive help through the Savior's grace, and resisting evil becomes easier.

Then we are born again of the Spirit when we receive the gift of the Holy Ghost. This third Member of the Godhead can influence whomever He chooses, but the right to have His constant companionship comes only through formal confirmation after baptism.

Baptism and receiving the gift of the Holy Ghost do not by themselves punch our ticket and guarantee entry into the celestial kingdom. They but open the gate to that eventual goal; getting there depends upon our faithfulness.

Number 4: Saved from ignorance. Christ's teachings bring us out of darkness and ignorance. Devout Mormons constantly study His life and teachings because such knowledge builds faith and protects us from evil.

Number 5: Saved from spiritual death. That is, every person who has not committed an unpardonable sin (intentional, premeditated murder, or has perfect knowledge of the Savior and then denies it) will receive one of the three kingdoms of glory. Everyone is saved to a different level of joy based on obedience to the laws and ordinances Christ established.

Number 6: Saved by being exalted. Exaltation means being in God's presence and living the life that God lives. It is the highest level within the celestial kingdom.

Therefore, who is saved depends upon which of the above six definitions one wants to discuss. All religions play certain roles, but only authorized Christianity can open the doors to the celestial kingdom.

CHAPTER 11

"Mormons Believe They Can Have Their Own Planet"

M akes us sound like a bunch of Trekkies, doesn't it?

When we bother to reply, we point to the Savior's statement that all things God has are His (Christ's), and Paul's statement that all of Christ's followers are joint heirs with Him.[43]   Presumably His estate includes planets.

Why would a group, viewed by 81% of its fellow citizens as intelligent and by 75% as well educated, come up with such a nutty idea? Unless, of course, it is an exaggeration of what, in a different light, is compelling logic.

The planet mockery arises from a speculative distortion from these interconnected beliefs:

- Christ has commanded all of us to become perfect even as our Father in heaven is perfect.[44] He would not have given us that commandment if it were not possible, but through His grace and our effort, it is.

- God wants His children to become perfect, to be exalted, and live the life that He lives. He desires to give us all that He has. This includes the blessing of having posterity forever.

- God has created worlds without number and continues to create them. His work is to bring to pass the happiness and eternal life of His children. He allows His children to help Him in His work, including assigning them stewardships.

Christ has commanded all mankind here on earth to love, serve, and help one another. We take that seriously in the church in that we are given assignments, stewardships, and responsibilities. The person who is faithful in handling small things will be assigned larger responsibilities. Thus, we grow and progress.

The same pattern will hold after this life. We will be given assignments and stewardships commensurate with our growing abilities. This is the concept of eternal progression.

Our critics take these concepts of eternal progression and exaltation, and sensationalize them into the claim that we believe we will have our own planet.

We do not know the details of what your or my stewardships may be after this life. Anything is possible. As a bishop, I had a stewardship for those living in a particular geographic area. It was my duty to teach, care for, and help them – to bring about God's plan for their progress and happiness. In my way of thinking, it is entirely possible in the hereafter for God to assign someone similar responsibilities to help His children in a specified location. If that's what our critics mean by "having our own planet," so be it. I reject their debasing sensationalism.

The most important thing is that whatever God has in store for mankind is made possible through the atonement of Jesus Christ. And that is the gift and power we must learn to use and appreciate more than we do.

The Blessings From Christ's Atonement

In my opinion, Christians of all denominations, including mine, do not ponder sufficiently what Christ's atonement actually means. While it is a common word in the Old Testament, *atonement* is mentioned only once in the New Testament, and its full meaning escapes many today.

Consider the word as if pronounced "at-one-ment" and its inherent meaning of reconciliation becomes more apparent. It is the process of becoming "at one with," or reconciled to, another. Its meaning is illuminated through the blessings Christ's atonement provides.

Through the fall of Adam, we became subject to two deaths – a spiritual separation from God and a physical separation of body and spirit. Through Christ's atoning sacrifice both deaths can be overcome.

We cannot imagine all that God has prepared for those who love Him

---

The first blessing of the atonement, therefore, is the resurrection, which is the restoration or reconciliation of body and spirit. Each person who has ever lived will have his or her body and spirit reunited. Because Christ triumphed over physical death, so will we. And it is a free gift to everyone requiring no effort on our part. Yes, even for Hitler and Mao.

The second blessing is the power to overcome spiritual death, which is the separation of man from God. When God unveiled His plan before we came to this earth, it was obvious that none of us would make it back on our own. We had not progressed enough to be perfect. We would make mistakes, we would sin, we would break commandments. Where there is a law, there is a punishment – there is justice to be paid. But, being imperfect, we would be incapable of purging those mistakes ourselves. And inasmuch as no unclean thing can live in God's presence, we would have been stuck if no perfect Being came to pay the price of our mistakes for us. That is why, among His many titles and names, Christ is called the Redeemer.

But the full power of this blessing requires us to do something as well. We Mormons believe that for the spiritual death to be overcome, we must enter into a covenant (that is, make promises) with Christ that boils down to His two-way proposition:

I will pay for your sins and you follow my commandments.

If we want to have all that *God* has, as He has offered to all mankind, then we must give all that *we* have.

Consider this reasoning: If the Lord overcame both physical and spiritual deaths for us and we had to do nothing but say thanks, would we be motivated to change our lives and become more Christ-like? Not very likely. Gratitude might prod us to live a better life for a while, but not as much as having the success of the endeavor conditioned upon our doing all we can to live His commandments.

Thus it is our belief that we must live His commandments (effort), and must recognize and repent of our sins (change). Then, when we nonetheless make mistakes and cannot pay the perfect price as He did, His grace will make up the shortfall. He stands ready to extend His mercy and grace, but why should He do it for lazy freeloaders who aren't willing to keep His commandments?

He has already given us one free gift and some complain because they aren't given two.

After these two great blessings comes the ultimate blessing – exaltation – and it throws our critics into a tizzy. It means that Christ provides the enabling power that can exalt us to the status of a god. (Go ahead, read it again, but note the small "g".)

Does exaltation mean that we can become equal to God? Absolutely not! Does it mean that we can become perfect like God? Yes. We didn't make up that doctrine out in the boonies of the Utah desert. That glimpse of the possible – to be perfect even as our Father in Heaven is perfect – comes from the Savior, as I have already noted.

> ## Perfection
>
> We can become perfect just as God is perfect.
>
> Yes   18%
> No   79
>
> The word *perfect* in Christ's admonition can also be translated from the Greek as *complete*. Either way, it is what God is and it is what He and Christ want all of us to be.

At the present time, however, only 18% believe as we do on this issue.

Complexity and Rewards

In graduate school, all of my roommates were in the hard sciences. Each evening, we would return from our classes to the big house we rented together and as they discussed their elegant mathematical models, I had to content myself with frequencies, percentages, and mundane statistical manipulations. The contrast was a point of humor with them.

One day I asked a roommate how many variables he had to measure to be able to confidently predict how the material he was studying would react. Three, he said: time, pressure, and temperature. I replied that in my field of study, predictive power from only three variables would be a miracle.

In the polling business, we study the most fascinating and complex subject matter ever created – the human being. The number of traits, characteristics, opinions, attitudes, values, feelings, knowledge, hopes, etc. is staggering, which makes predicting behavior dicey, but exciting nonetheless.

During the 1980 campaign between Ronald Reagan and Jimmy Carter, one of our interviewers came into my office to tell me about a survey interview the previous evening. The voter, it seemed, was a die-hard Reagan fan. High image marks for Reagan, low ones for Carter. Same with issues – she was solid on Reagan's positions and disparaged Carter's. Then came the vote: "If the election for president were held today, would you vote for Ronald Reagan, Republican, or Jimmy Carter, Democrat?" The lady said she would vote for Carter. My interviewer was floored. The reason? "Well, everyone knows that every president elected in a year that ends with a zero has died in office. And I love Ronald Reagan too much to see him die in office."

Just when you think you can predict behavior....

My point is that the complexity of mankind necessarily leads to variability in the final grades, if you will, that we receive for this test on earth. Consider this logic chain:

- Each individual is immensely complex.

- Within humanity are infinite variations of people.

- Given all the variations in humanity *here*, why would these variations not remain with us when we go *there*, to the "other side"?

- Whatever position a person occupies on whatever scales God will eventually use to judge us, there will be someone who is greater ... and another one greater still. We will be lined up from greatest to the least.

- Why should the rewards for how well we lived our lives on earth be any less scaled?

How could it possibly be fair to divide complex humanity into a heaven-or-hell existence, no variations within those two categories allowed? Would it be fair to give the person in the 51st percentile the same reward as the person in the 99th? Or the person in the 49th percentile the same punishment meted to the lowest? Should everyone be relegated to a simple pass/fail grade?

Christ's teachings are comforting on this point. We believe He was illustrating that there are gradations in the hereafter when He told His followers, "In my Father's house are many mansions."[45] There are gradations and it is not only okay to aspire to the top one, it is commanded. It is what Christ referred to when he said not to be taken in by earthly things, but to lay up treasures in heaven.[46]

In this materialistic world where people grub for the hottest car, the finest clothes, and the biggest house, why do a few people criticize Mormons for having more sublime aspirations for the next world?

To emphasize what should be our goal in life, Christ taught that we cannot even imagine what God has prepared for those who love Him,[47] which we do by keeping His commandments. We know at a minimum that it means all of mankind can become joint heirs with Christ of all that the Father has given to Him. Everything.

The interesting point is that almost all Christians believe that an unimaginable glory awaits the faithful. We Mormons simply have a name for it ... exaltation.

Planets and all, I guess.

CHAPTER 12

"Mormons Have Secret Temples and Magic Underwear"

There is no religious belief that cannot somehow be made to look weird.

Sophists scorn religious ceremonies as shallow, anesthetizing gibberish for the superstitious. They can't believe that thinking people can be religious.

They have it exactly backwards. I believe that non-religious people are missing out on a deeper intellect that is honed in the Lord's temples.

The first thing to understand about temples is that they have always been an integral part of Christianity.

As explained earlier, it does not make sense that Adam and Eve would have been taught differing religions – one from God the Father and the other from Jesus Christ, the Son. They were taught Christianity, and the first thing they did when they were booted out of the Garden of Eden was build an altar at which they prayed and on which they offered sacrifices, as we believe God directed them. Altars since then have always been at the center of temple worship. An altar can exist without surrounding walls, but a temple isn't a temple without an altar.

Temples, whether an actual structure or a secluded location, are to be "places apart" from everyday life – a place to retreat from the cares, temptations, and profane eyes of the world and to commune with Deity. (The Latin word *templum* means exactly that: a place cut off, or apart – what we call a sacred place.)

At times, temple worship was restricted to those who held a special priesthood, such as the tribe of Levi, while at other times it has been accessible to all who are worthy, practicing followers of the Lord.

The purpose of temples throughout history is to focus us on Christ, the Messiah – His mission, atonement, and resurrection – and teach His followers the mysteries of the Kingdom of God.

Deep knowledge indeed.

The Temple in Christ's Time

Just as Christ taught with parables during his earthly sojourn, so similarly did He establish a symbol-rich environment in His temples so His followers could learn to comprehend the deeper things for which words are inadequate.

These symbols existed in Solomon's temple, the most famous in history and one of the most ornate buildings ever constructed. It remained a place of true worship of the Lord for about 50 years, and then the sacred rituals and symbols were scattered to the world as Israel drifted from her God. In fact, there is nothing in temple worship – clothing, altars, symbols, etc. – that cannot be found in one or more religions of the world, Christian and non-Christian alike.

The temple of Solomon, built around 1000 BC, was destroyed when the Babylonians under Nebuchadnezzar II conquered Jerusalem. It was rebuilt twice, once by Zerubbabel around 516 BC after the return of the Jews from captivity, and again in 16 BC by Herod, a Roman puppet ruler, trying to ingratiate himself with the Jewish people.

Temples are the Lord's university

Though the temple at the time of Christ was not functioning according to God's original intent, the Savior nonetheless recognized it as His Father's house and one fine day made life rough for the moneychangers who had turned it into a temple of commerce.

Early Christian texts such as the Nag Hammadi library reference elements of temple worship and leave little doubt that the temple ceremony, with its attendant practice of making covenants or promises with the Lord, was practiced by Christ's disciples following His death and resurrection.[48]

The differences between temple worship before and after Christ result from the fulfillment of the Law of Moses and the establishment of the higher law brought by Christ. The temple under Mosaic Law included the sacrifice of animals – unblemished first-born bullocks, sheep, etc. – as a symbol of and focus on the coming of the sinless Messiah and His sacrifice for our sins. Once Jesus Christ had accomplished this great atonement, there was obviously no need for further symbolism through the shedding of blood. Members of the church today symbolically place upon the altar a broken heart and a contrite spirit instead.

As a symbol of this transition, the rending of the veil at the moment of Christ's death on the cross signified that the Law of Moses had been fulfilled. No longer would only one priest be allowed into the temple. Temple worship would be open to all worthy disciples of the Lord Jesus Christ.

Temples Today

We Mormons construct two main types of buildings. We have 20,000 places of worship we call meetinghouses or churches – places for our regular Sunday worship services. We also have, as of the summer of 2011, 134 temples worldwide for special worship services and ceremonies.

Image Traits	
Mormons ...	
Are superstitious	26%
Do weird things in their temples	19%

We believe that every person who has ever lived must be given the opportunity to enter into an agreement with our Savior – we call it a covenant – whereby the person promises to live His commandments and the person in return receives blessings. That is why we perform these ordinances vicariously, such as baptism, for those who lived and died without hearing Christ's teachings.

As we perform these ceremonies and ordinances for those who have passed away, we get deeper insights into what Christ has done for us and what lies ahead if we are true to the promises we have made.

Temples are places of education, inspiration, and revelation where the most profound intellectual activity can be experienced. Universities look shabby by comparison. This is where, with our spiritual intellect, we commune with that great Being who comprehends all things.

Against this activity, other forms of intellectualism are child's play.

Specifics

It is not unusual for members of any religion to hesitate to talk casually about things they hold sacred. And decent people respect such. So I have been both amazed and saddened at the ridiculous rumors spread about us and our temples, some so absurd and malicious they are beneath contempt and unworthy of response.

People who have legitimate questions and are open-minded, however, deserve to hear our answers.

Here are short explanations of various elements of temple worship.

- **Altars**. We do nothing at the altars except kneel to pray, make promises to God, get married, and seal families together for eternity, much in common with other faiths that use altars.

- **Anointing**. The use of pure olive oil to anoint the head of one who is to receive a blessing was a common practice in both Old and New Testament times.[49]

- **Baptism**. We baptize by immersion, as do many other religions. In temples, we baptize by proxy (that is, someone standing in for a deceased person) those who have passed away without having been baptized by one having the authority to do so. Records tell us early Christians in Corinth performed this ordinance as well.[50]

- **Clothing**. In temples, we dress in white. For certain ceremonies we also don additional vestments such as robes and head coverings. It's described in Exodus.[51]

- **Endowment**. A university endowment is a gift of money. A temple endowment is a gift of power – power to overcome evil, and through our faithfulness and the grace of Christ someday live in God's presence. In the endowment ceremony, the history of mankind is presented and we pause periodically to make covenants – honesty, morality, and service – with the Lord.

- **Garments**. Priests and officers in many religions wear outwardly visible priestly clothing. We also have priestly raiment, but we wear ours under our street clothing, and grant such privilege to all worthy members, men and women alike, not solely our leaders. The world mocks what they call our magic underwear. There's nothing magic about them at all. The temple garment serves to remind us of our promises to God and His Son. Maybe the world just thinks it is seeing magic when people resist evil and live good lives.

- **Instruction**. Every religion offers advanced classes for those who want to hear and learn more than a Sunday sermon. We do the same. Temples are dedicated as the House of the Lord where we believe His spirit can be felt – His university, if you will. We go to be taught in a quiet, reverent setting the advanced topics of Christ's gospel, spirit to spirit.

- **Marriages**. Christ gave Peter the sealing power, the power to bind in heaven as on earth. This same sealing power is found in our temples today. It is administered to seal husbands and wives together in marriages that, if they are faithful, will last beyond this life – we use the phrase "marriage for time and eternity." The sealing power is also used to seal children to parents, generation after generation.

- **Prayer**. No surprise here. We pray in temples the same way the Savior prayed with His apostles.

- **Proxy ordinances**. We do not believe that time and place of birth exclude any of God's children from blessings that God gives to other children. Many have lived and died without ever having heard of Jesus Christ. Therefore, in temples we perform by proxy all of the ordinances – baptism, confirmation, endowment, and sealing – that we believe God wants all of us to receive. Such ordinances provide the deceased with an option; they are not forced to accept anything. We work, they decide.

- **Symbols**. Christ taught through parables, metaphors, and symbols so people had to think deeply to grasp the richness of His doctrine. It is the same in His temples. To read a purloined script of our temple ceremony and claim to understand the symbols is like taking a picture of a bank and claiming to understand economics.

- **Veil.** The veil of the temple throughout history has been a symbol of the separation of this life from the next.

- **Washing.** Christ washed the feet of His apostles at the sacrament of the Last Supper. Similarly, those attending the temple are washed symbolically, not literally, prior to receiving the blessing of the endowment.

As you can see, elements of the temple are commonly found here and there in other religions. We have them together in one place.

The deeper question is this: Why don't other Christian religions have temples – these special places, more sacred than the buildings used for general worship, where all the power and blessings that Christ provided for His followers in New Testament times can be received? Temples belong to Christianity as much as the sacrament of the Lord's Supper, the atonement, and the resurrection.

The weird Christian religion is not the one *with* temples; it's the one *without* them.

CHAPTER 13

"Mormons Believe Crazy Things"

What if there were a story that God had appeared to someone in 580 BC, and another story that three men were tossed into a furnace in 1820 AD but weren't burned?

Which story would people today believe is the crazy one?

Dr. Jan Shipps, perhaps the most prominent non-Mormon scholar on Mormonism, observed: "Mormonism is a really complex theological system. All its parts fit together beautifully. But if you just know a little bit about one of them, or part of them, it seems weird."[52]

My recent survey found that 24% view Mormons as weird and 35% say that we believe crazy things. This tracks with the 2008 survey in which we gave people the choice of labeling Mormons as nice or wacky, and with reasonable or irrational beliefs:

Nice people with reasonable beliefs	53%
Nice people with irrational beliefs	31
Wacky people with reasonable beliefs	7
Wacky people with irrational beliefs	3

Nice, reasonable, irrational, and wacky – 84-60-34-10 in that order.

This is a common pattern throughout my research. Strong majorities in the 70- and 80-percent range attribute positive traits to Mormons such as nice, honest, spiritual, well-educated, intelligent, friendly, etc., while 20% to 35% focus on the negatives and feel criticisms are justified.

Let's summarize Mormon beliefs, weird and crazy though some may claim them to be.

1. Adam and Eve

Mormons believe that Adam and Eve were actual human beings, created in the image of God, the first man and woman of our species on the earth. We believe they ate forbidden fruit that caused death to come into the world, and that Adam lived to be over 900 years old before he died.

2. The Flood

Mormons believe that a major flood once covered at least a sizeable part of the earth. But before it did, God directed a man to build a big boat, stock it with animals, and sail away while the waters killed off wicked people.

3. The Exodus

Mormons believe that the people of Israel were led out of Egypt by a man named Moses. We believe that through God's power, the Red Sea was parted long enough to allow thousands of them to cross over on dry ground. When they were all safe on the other side, the waters came back together and drowned the world's then-largest army.

And talk about room service. Mormons believe that every morning the people of Israel would wake up and find their food on the ground ready to eat. When they tired of eating this bread-like substance and complained about never having meat to eat, the Lord sent so many quail to fall into their camp that they were piled up three feet deep. (You want meat; I'll show you meat.)

4. Old Testament Events

Mormons believe that God told a man to offer his son as a sacrifice, but then sent an angel to stop him ... that a boy killed an eight-foot giant with a stone and a slingshot ... that trumpets brought down the walls of a great city ... that men were shoved into a furnace but were not burned ... that a man was tossed into a den of hungry lions and the lions refused to eat him ... that another man was fed by a raven ... that a donkey talked ... that an ax floated ... that a widow had a barrel of flour and container of oil that never ran out ... that a man commanded the sun to stand still so he could finish a battle ... that a man commanded it not to rain for three years and it didn't... and on and on. Whew.

Mormons believe all these weird things.

5. Christ's Miracles

Mormons believe Jesus Christ turned water into wine ... raised people from the dead ... fed 5000 people with five loaves of bread and two fishes ... healed lepers ... caused the lame to walk, the blind to see, the deaf to hear ... walked on water ... told Peter how to catch a fish that would have a coin in it so taxes could be paid ... reattached the ear of a Roman servant ... among many other miracles.

Mormons believe He had power over death, that He voluntarily laid down His life as a ransom for all mankind, and that He then picked it up again as a resurrected Being. We believe He continued to appear before hundreds of people and even walked through walls.

Why should time determine whether something is or is not believable?

---

6. Visions and Visitations

Mormons believe that both God the Father and Jesus Christ appeared to Joseph Smith in a vision and called him to be a prophet of God. We also believe Joseph Smith received visitations and instruction from John the Baptist; Peter, James, and John; Moroni, a Christian prophet who lived on the American continent about 400 AD; Moses; Elijah; Elias; and many other prophets who once lived on the earth.

Mormons further believe that the aforementioned Moroni delivered to Joseph Smith an ancient record engraved on metallic pages (golden plates) that Joseph translated through the power of God. This translation is known today as the Book of Mormon, another verification or witness that Jesus Christ is truly the Son of God, the Messiah who will come to the earth again, this time in great glory.

Mormons believe God still speaks to prophets today to help His children.

7. Temples

Mormons believe that temples are sanctuaries where people can draw closer to God, a purpose of temples from Adam on down through history. We believe that in such temples, covenants (promises) can be made that will last for eternity, such as marriage. In today's temples, Mormons make promises of honesty, morality, and service and are clothed in priestly raiment, as has always been the case in God's temples from Old Testament times to today. In fact, many religions have copied practices or clothing from the ancient original temples.

8. Fairness

Mormons believe it is not fair to consign to hell all children and others who were not baptized before they died. We believe that all of God's children will have the opportunity to hear Christ's gospel, which they can then accept or reject. We perform baptisms for such people in our temples, a practice known as baptism for the dead that early Christians also performed.

9. Pre-Earthly Life

Mormons believe man is co-eternal (but not co-equal) with God, that we have always existed, that we were not created out of nothing, and that we have lived for eternities, and will live for eternity. We believe that God created us in the sense of organizing our elements, and that He is the Father of our spirits. We believe further that a person on earth today is composed of two parts – a physical body and a spirit, and that this spirit is of a refined, yet tangible, matter. When the body dies, the spirit continues to live.

10. A Test and Our Destiny

Mormons believe that all people came to earth to learn the difference between good and evil, and to be tested. We believe that Jesus Christ, God's Firstborn and Only Begotten Son in the flesh, was chosen to be the Redeemer of the world and through His sacrifice atone for our sins. We believe that Lucifer, an advanced spirit child of God, rebelled and became Satan, the embodiment of evil. We believe that we will continue to live after we leave this earth life, and that one day all of God's children who have inhabited a mortal body will be resurrected, their spirits permanently reunited with their bodies, never to die again.

Just as every parent wants his or her children to become the best they can be, God our Father expects the same of us. Therefore, Mormons believe that man has the potential to become perfect through the grace of Jesus Christ.

We Mormons are a tempting punching bag for comedians looking for laughs.

We ask the world: If one happens to believe the first five things on the list above, as many Americans do, what is so laughable about the last five?

PART II

ANSWERS
ABOUT PEOPLE

CHAPTER 14

"Mormons Are Blind Followers and Don't Think for Themselves"

O ne could take offense at that, but I think it's amusing for all of the reasons that follow.

We Mormons often respond to these century-old slurs by pointing out such things as … our above-average education levels among second- and third-generation Mormons (many converts come from lower socio-economic strata but their children and grandchildren move up)[53] … the high percentage of Mormons who speak a second language … that Brigham Young University (98% LDS) ranks tenth in the nation in producing graduates who go on to earn doctorates[54] … and so on.

But there is a more interesting refutation. Such caricatures fade as more people come to understand that people of all faiths can tap into the knowledge we acquired when we lived with Heavenly Father before we came to this earth.

Deeper than logical intellect and our intuitive emotional intellect, it's called spiritual intellect.

My Stanford Days

Mind if I share a personal odyssey?

Even though I was a seventh-generation Mormon, had served a mission for the church and had graduated from BYU, it took five years in graduate school at Stanford for me to recognize how deep my beliefs had become.

Surrounded and challenged by 23 bright fellow students, I loved the mental tussles and the invigorating debates – which are easy to come by when you're the only Mormon, the only Republican, and the only conservative in the department.

But it all played out on a shallow plane. Something was missing.

Feelings? Spiritual stirrings? Impossible in an intellectual setting, pal. Can't be objectively dissected, measured, demonstrated – you know the drill.

Despite it all, I knew that I understood things that defied an objective proof – and that intellectual prowess by itself was insufficient to explain it.

There had to be more to us than our logical brain. Or even our emotional brain.

There had to be a deeper intellect at work.

Whence, Why, Whither

I don't recall the first time I heard that God is the Father of our spirits – that He created us spiritually (yes, with arms and legs, head and feet ... and **brain**) before we were sent to earth to inhabit a mortal body. All I knew as I grew up was that I knew it was right. It was familiar to me and it made sense. And knowing where we came from is a pre-requisite to working through the questions that have occupied philosophers for centuries – why we're here and where we're going.

I mulled those concepts a lot. If we lived with God before we were sent to this earth, what did we do all day long? Play on our lyres? Skip stones on some celestial pond? Bounce from cloud to cloud?

No, we were learning. Conversations for sure. Maybe classrooms. Progressing. Trying to emulate our Father.

And then, we Mormons believe, a curtain was drawn across our memories of that pre-earthly existence, so that this earth life, intentionally designed so things would go wrong, could be a test.

Hmmm. So if we had billions of years of learning, where might all that knowledge be stored today? Back upstairs in some safe-deposit box?

No. We brought it with us, somehow imprinted on our spiritual brain.

Connecting the Dots

Can we tap into that trove of knowledge here? Absolutely. But it cannot be done with our surface intellect alone.

Some neuroscientists have distinguished between the rational brain and the emotional brain, and have demonstrated that the emotional brain can recognize patterns more quickly than can the rational brain – the quarterback who senses more than he can articulate that it would not be wise to throw to his wide receiver, or the British sailor in the first Gulf War who felt that the blip on his radar was a Silkworm missile and not a friendly returning A-6 and shot it down, thus saving the battleship USS Missouri, because things "didn't feel right." (Imagine giving *that* explanation to a Navy captain.)[55]

The rational brain can handle four variables simultaneously, whereas the emotional brain can accommodate upwards of 20 variables at the same time. If all 20 variables don't line up in an expected way, the brain does not release dopamine, the feel-good neurotransmitter, and the person feels that something must be amiss. Which is why the quarterback doesn't throw to his wide receiver, but can't explain it until he later looks at the full-view video of the play and sees that the safety was creeping up, or the linebacker was falling back into coverage. His emotional brain detected it, not his rational.[56]

So if there is a more discerning emotional mind behind the rational mind, what might be behind even that? How deep does it go? And how many variables can it handle simultaneously?

Each person has three intellects – the rational, the emotional, and the spiritual

---

My experiences convince me that we have at least three levels of intellect – a rational brain, an emotional brain, and a spiritual brain. We discover truths at each level by connecting the dots, by recognizing patterns that coincide with other patterns we have previously satisfied ourselves are true.

While the workings of the rational brain allow us to objectively demonstrate to others what we deduce to be true, truths at the emotional and spiritual level must be experienced. They cannot be objectively proved to an outsider who has not experimented with the patterns or connected the dots for himself.

In my own case, why did new statements and claims strike me as familiar when they had never been grist for my rational mind? Why did certain patterns almost scream, "True!" even before I could explain them? Why did statements, principles, and insights strike me as things that I have always known? To use an overworked word, why did they resonate?

It is because they were patterns I had already seen in another sphere.

They came with me to this frail existence, and though they are buried on the spiritual side of my three-and-a-half pound hunk of gray matter, they pop through often enough to tell me that there is so much more truth waiting to be learned (re-learned, actually) and applied if I push beyond today's intellectualism, as it is currently championed.

Aristotle said that an eye for similarities is the mark of genius. It necessarily follows that anyone can become a spiritual genius by learning how to recognize the eternal truths that are already inside us.

That's the beauty of intellect in the spiritual dimension: a high traditional IQ is not a pre-requisite.

Comprehending

We use the word *logic* to describe the process of the rational brain.

We use the word *feelings* to describe the process of the emotional brain.

But neither word does justice to the product of the spiritual brain. The best word for this intellectual process is *comprehension*.

Logic, feelings, comprehension. All appropriate in their sphere, but in the eternal scheme of things I describe them as the puny, the interesting, and the deep.

When dots get connected on this deep intellectual spiritual plane, words and even symbols are rarely the transferring mechanism, but rather a silent wholesale transfer of knowing as if in a flash of inspiration. One minute, comprehension eludes us, and in the next minute the vistas of eternity on the topic of our inquiry are opened to us. We see, we grasp, we discern, we sense, we feel … we know. Some have even used the word *taste* to describe it. We simply *comprehend* as spirit connects with spirit – as what was learned in the pre-earthly spirit world is manifest to our understanding in this world.

Learn it there, comprehend it here – the things the finite mind alone cannot wrap itself around.

Dig Deeper

Let me directly address my intellectual friends of high mental megahertz:

You assume that the logical mind is man's dominant power. In reality it is only the beginning of the power of learning and comprehension that the whole man – mind, feelings, and spirit – can possess.

Sadly, too many of you are comfortable staying on the finite plane and never invest the effort and purity of thought that are necessary to progress to the infinite plane.

You have been on earth for a few decades and have accomplished noteworthy things with your brain. You have read, studied, discussed, debated, and manipulated theories until there's bovine migration, all of which have led to insights and discoveries. This is good and laudable as God intended.

But quickness of intellect is only one component of intelligence. The greater intellectual reward takes place in a deep introspective world invisible to those unwilling to expend the intellectual effort to stretch their minds beyond the applause of men.

Therefore, you cannot stop on this surface plane, no matter how interesting you may think it is. If you haven't experienced the spiritual-intellectual process, you're in for a treat – which may be the reason why Mormons with college degrees or higher are more religiously active and faithful in their religion than similarly educated men and women are in other religions.[57]

The God of this universe expects you and me and all of His children to go beyond the rational and emotional minds and deepen our intellectual efforts. God invites us to work on this profound spiritual-intellectual plane so that someday we may achieve His goal for us – to comprehend all things, past, present, and future, just as He does.

It's fun, it's exhilarating, it's challenging, and it's amazingly satisfying. Once you experience it, you will never again view the spiritual as inferior to your brand of intellectualism.

The Bicycle Light

With that explanation of the spiritual-intellectual process as background, let's now return to the charge that Mormons are unthinkingly and blindly obedient.

If God personally appeared to me and told me to do something, I would not be blindly obedient if I did it. Rather, I would be knowingly obedient because I would know that it came from God. But let's say the counsel comes from a church leader who says that it is God's desire that I do something. What then? How do I determine whether it is legitimate counsel or someone invoking God's name for selfish purposes?

This discovery process has two parts: field experiments and personal revelation.

The experiment aspect has a parallel to my humble mode of transportation as a missionary in Germany. My bicycle was not equipped with a battery-powered headlight, but rather a dynamo that spun when positioned against the side of a moving front tire, thus generating electricity that powered the light. The catch: no light unless I was moving.

Image Traits

Mormons are …

Intelligent	81%
Spiritual	81%
Well-educated	75%
Encouraged to think for themselves	45%
Blind followers	37%
Brainwashed	33%
Gullible	24%

It took faith to put the bike in motion, especially on an unlit path between two villages at night when we rested at the top of a hill before continuing. I had to take an action; I had to conduct a small experiment.

Following the prophets, past and present, is like pushing off into that darkness. Even if I am not well versed on the topic at hand, I am confident that as I push into the darkness, the light will come on and I will see the same path the prophet sees. Is that blind obedience? Not at all. It is a *field experiment*. And experiments always contain uncertainty until they fully unfold. I put directions to the test by acting on them, and have come to trust from past experiments that the light will come on and I will know the reasons behind the counsel.

The second aspect is personal revelation. I as a simple member have every right to tap into the same information source as the giver of the counsel.

Before I can ask for a *personal revelation* on the matter, however, I must invest effort. I must do my homework. As I push myself to the deeper spiritual-intellectual plane, my meditating mind looks for similarities between the counsel and patterns I have previously experienced are true. Then I ask for verification – it's called prayer.

This process of personal revelation is "our answer to the charge that Latter-day Saints follow their leaders out of 'blind obedience,'" as one leader put it. "[W]e are all privileged and encouraged to confirm their [the prophets'] teachings by prayerfully seeking and receiving revelatory confirmation directly from God."[58]

Spiritual intellect is the mechanism through which we receive this revelatory confirmation, a way to double-check and verify that counsel from prophets and apostles is correct. We have found the process – God commanding, prophets relaying, and members verifying – to be sound.

Available to All

This learned ability has been available forever.

Christ spoke in parables to both friends and enemies in Jerusalem. His followers grasped what He was teaching because they were tracking on a deeper level. But his enemies were baffled; they were those who seeing did not see, and hearing did not understand.[59] They were strangers to spiritual intellect.

So what appears to the world to be stupid may instead be deep and profound. What appears to be blind following may turn out to be well-informed discipleship. All because of spiritual intellect and its attendant personal revelation.

And talk about immediate benefits. Obedience to God's commandments and the directions of His prophets produces purer minds because they're not cluttered with improper images and hateful thoughts. Such minds of necessity are more fertile and creative. Insights come easier, inspiration more quickly, and more gets done.

I firmly believe that a pure mind with a 125 IQ can grasp and accomplish more than an impure mind at 150.

Obedience and comprehension go hand in hand.

CHAPTER 15

"Mormons Practice Polygamy"

S urveys indicate that the facts about polygamy are among the top
three things people want to know about Mormons.

So here are the facts: yes we did and no we don't.

The way I look at polygamy is that such an assignment from God may
not have been as bad as being commanded to build an ark in a back-
yard hundreds of miles from an ocean, but it comes close.

There were times in biblical history when God commanded polygamy
be practiced, as with Abraham and Jacob, and times when He did
not.[60]   Similarly, during the 19th century, there was about a 50-year
period when God commanded specific church members to practice
it.[61] (We joke that when Brigham Young finished work each day, he
could go home in any direction.)   Then in 1890, three years after
Congress passed the Edmunds-Tucker Act outlawing the practice,
God commanded that it cease.[62]

Thus, we do not practice polygamy today, even though 46% of
Americans still believe we do and only 14% are definitely sure that we
do not. Strange, isn't it, in an age of instant information.

> ## Mormons and Polygamy
>
> "Do Mormons practice polygamy?"
>
> | | |
> |---|---|
> | Definitely Yes | 15% |
> | Probably Yes | 31 |
> | Probably No | 18 |
> | **Definitely No** | **14** |
> | Don't know | 22 |
>
> Uncertainty level: 86%

At the time it was sanctioned by the church, only a minor percentage ever practiced it and one prominent member who did not was Reed Smoot, elected to the U.S. Senate in 1902, not long after Utah was admitted to the Union in 1896. Polygamy still being a controversial issue, many senators opposed seating him. The debate continued until 1907 when Senator Boies Penrose of Pennsylvania tipped the scales for Smoot when he said, looking directly at more than one philandering Senator, "I would rather have seated beside me in this chamber a polygamist who doesn't polyg than a monogamist who doesn't monog."[63]

Reasons

Several reasons have been proffered why God commanded this practice:

- Given the persecution of the church, there was an imbalance between men and women, and more women needed to be cared for, especially as the church transplanted itself from Illinois to the Utah desert.

- Because original Christianity needed to be re-established to be the forerunner for the Second Coming of the Savior in all countries, there was a need to jump-start its growth.

- We believe that our religion is the restoration of all things, and that all blessings and practices that were had in previous eras are to be restored or re-established in our day. This includes the priesthood, the power to conduct temple ordinances, the power to put in motion the gathering of Israel to their ancient homeland, and would then, of course, have to include the practice of polygamy, of short duration though it was.

Any member of our church found in a polygamous marriage is excommunicated

Maybe it was one of the above, none of the above, or a combination. To my knowledge, God has not revealed His full reasoning on the matter. Contrary to the salacious charges against the practitioners, it should be obvious that if all a man wanted was more sexual gratification, the world offers easier ways than taking on the financial and emotional burdens of a second wife and family.

Faith Communities and Breakaway Groups

Much of the confusion about Mormons and polygamy arises when people identify us with the breakaway groups from our church, over 150 of them, some of which practice polygamy. These groups use names that cleverly suggest a legitimate relationship with us:

- The Fundamentalist Church of Jesus Christ of Latter-day Saints

- The True and Living Church of Jesus Christ of Saints of the Last Days

- Latter Day Church of Christ

- Church of the Lamb of God

- Apostolic United Brethren

- Righteous Branch of the Church of Jesus Christ of Latter-day Saints

- Church of Jesus Christ of Latter-day Saints and the Kingdom of God

But we have **absolutely nothing** to do with them, no matter how creative their names and no matter how many of our doctrines they may believe. And no matter how many HBO ads imply that *Big Love* is about Mormons.

I call it the faith-community fallacy.

For example, most people who aren't Baptists do not make a distinction between Southern Baptists, Independent Baptists, and American Baptists – Baptists are Baptists, so they reason. But Baptists know the distinctions.

Similarly, how many non-Lutherans distinguish between Evangelical Lutherans and the Lutheran Church-Missouri Synod? Few. But Lutherans do.

Same with us. Those of other faiths unfairly lump us together with splinter groups as if we were one big Mormon faith community, or faith tradition, though we maintain they are no more part of us than Protestants are part of Catholicism.

Look at it this way. If I founded a church and called it the Fundamentalist Methodist Church, would that make me a Methodist? If I believed 90% of what true Methodists believe, but the other 10% was in considerable opposition to their doctrines, would Methodists accept me as part of their faith community? Doubtful.

We are all guilty of grouping people and denominations into faith communities, and we Mormons are just as guilty of such lumping as anyone else. While we are trying to be more accurate in how we categorize other religions, we hope others would be just as discerning about us. Just because someone puts the word "fundamentalist" or a similar word in front of the title of our church, one should not assume that group is a part of our faith community.

In fact, we are a one-denomination faith family. If we excommunicate a member for polygamy and he starts his own church, you better believe he is not a part of us, no matter how many copies of the Book of Mormon he has on his shelf.

Monogamy Only

In short, sometimes God commands His people to practice polygamy, as happened in Old Testament times, and sometimes, when man's laws make it difficult to carry out His commandments, the Lord has released His people from a previous directive because He has also commanded us to be subject to the laws of the lands in which we live.[64]

The President of the Church, Wilford Woodruff, announced the following in October of 1890:

> Inasmuch as laws have been enacted by Congress forbidding plural marriages, which laws have been pronounced constitutional by the court of last resort, I hereby declare my intention to submit to those laws, and to use my influence with the members of the Church over which I preside to have them do likewise.[65]

Some observers today call this a revelation of convenience, and say that man's laws trumped God's. I agree it looks that way on the surface, and government pressure obviously played its role. Those with boots on the ground at the time, however, would have continued polygamy despite being imprisoned by the government, as many were, had not the Lord used the events to impress upon the Latter-day Saints the significance of a more important practice – temple work.

Subsequent to the Official Declaration noted above, President Woodruff explained that he was shown in a vision what would happen to our temple work if polygamy continued. So the people would understand and support the decision, the Lord told him to ask them which was more important: to continue the practice of plural marriage (our name for polygamy) and suffer a stoppage in temple work, or to submit to the properly legislated and adjudicated law of the land? They got the picture.

This tells me that by the end of the 19th century, plural marriage had served its purposes, whatever they were, and that a higher goal was now to supplant the practice. It was time to focus on more important preparations for the Savior's Second Coming.

Therefore, monogamy is now the only authorized marriage practice in the LDS Church, as it has been for more than 120 years.

To give you an idea of how seriously we follow both the do's and the don'ts of God's commandments, if I wanted to be *quickly* excommunicated from my church, I would practice polygamy. That's because all other sins take longer.

Any member of our church found in a polygamous relationship is excommunicated. Period. A person has a better chance of keeping his membership if he's a monogamist who doesn't monog.

But that's against the rules, too.

CHAPTER 16

"Mormons Are Bigoted Homophobes"

How's that for a lovely compliment when all we want is to protect traditional marriage in a battle we did not initiate?

That there are two sexes screams that there must be a master plan.

We declare that marriage is God's institution, not man's. We believe that He has a master plan for His children and that gender is at its foundation.

Sure, if God had so intended, He could have had us grow on trees and drop to the ground as fully developed non-sex adults. But He didn't.

It is impossible to believe that such a master plan would not address the purpose of gender and provide for an agreement – marriage – between a man and a woman. Nor can we believe that such a solemn agreement would not be of critical importance to a commitment to nurture new life that may ensue.

So, should the establishment of a commitment to nurture and raise helpless infants be left to a happenstance, man-made agreement?

We ask whether it makes sense that the Creator of this master plan would leave to chance that man would stumble across the need for such an agreement some century in the future – that its creation and definition should be left to man-made governments?

No. Gender and the plan for marriage were created at the same time.

Gender and Inclinations

As explained earlier, we believe life is a test in a sphere of existence where things go wrong, and that inclinations and weaknesses are part of that test. Every person is guaranteed to have a weakness, a temptation, an inclination that God wants him or her to overcome. Struggling with such challenges strengthens and refines. It is part of God's plan for our growth.

Which is why we feel sadness when one of our brothers or sisters would rather indulge an inclination than conquer it.

Consider the word *gender*, a convenient concept the lesbian and gay community has made malleable. By last count, they claim seven types of genders and speak of gender fluidity. They assert that feelings rather than biological makeup determine one's sexuality, and that when one feels part of a newly invented gender category, one is justified acting accordingly – an excuse, in other words, not to overcome the inclinations.

The origin of the word, however, does not support the way they use it. Never more than a dual-category construct, gender came into vogue in early 20th century genteel company as an equivalent substitute for the word sex, which had taken on erotic qualities.[66] Instead of a polite stand-in for "sex of a human being," gender has now been imbued with social traits, making it easier to accommodate trendy definitions of the day.

We stand in opposition to the infinitely expandable definition of gender proclaimed by same-sex marriage proponents. We maintain that God created only two genders. We further state that same-sex attractions by themselves are *not* sinful, but *are if acted upon*.

Right to the Institution

Marriage is both a legal contract as well as an institution. Man's legal authority on earth can and must determine arrangements necessary for societal order, such as financial matters and the settling of disputes, but cannot trump an institution, founded before this world was, that specifically identifies the genders of the parties.

God and Marriage

"Do you believe that the institution of marriage was …"

Created by God	58%
Created by man	40

"If God made His opinion known, do you feel He would or would not expand the definition of marriage to include same-sex marriage?"

He would	29%
He would not	58

We believe that God, not man, created the institution of marriage and He alone can change it.

Compare marriage to a church. The Catholics, as one example, believe their church came from God, that it was not created by man. Now suppose someone who is not a Catholic says to the Pope, "I like your church and want to become part of it. But I want you to change your liturgy and commandments to accommodate my behavior, which you happen to oppose."

Fat chance. No church that believes their institution came from God would allow an outsider to change it.

Yet this is exactly the same demand made by proponents of same-sex marriage. Those who believe marriage was created by God, and is the natural pairing of two genders, are being told, "*You* must accommodate *me* into *your* institution on *my* terms!" Unbelievable.

Are we unreasonable if we say, "Are you serious?" In the example above, if the Catholic Church turns down the petitioner, does he have the right to form his own church? Absolutely. Does he have the right to call it the Catholic Church? Absolutely not.

Same thing with marriage.

Demonizing

One of the oldest ploys in public debate is to demonize one's opponent by equating disagreement with hatred – that if someone disagrees with you, that person must be hateful and bigoted. It is the attempt to win by sympathy what one fails to win on the merits.

Because the LDS Church strongly disagrees with same-sex marriage, Mormons have been called some imaginative names, bigot being one of the milder ones. It's simply the latest version of "If A disagrees with B, A is correct; if B disagrees with A, B is hateful."

We counsel our members not to respond in kind, just as in other disagreements we may have. For example, we may disagree with Catholics about infant baptism, but we don't hate them. We may disagree with evangelicals about the definition of grace, but we don't hate them. We may disagree with Jews about who Christ is, but we don't hate them. Disagreement does not mean hatred.

The LGBT (lesbian, gay, bisexual, transgender) community will reply that doctrinal differences are one thing, but "taking away a right" is another matter.

Let's examine that assumptive point of view.

Role of Government

First, marriage either came from God or from man. If God created it, where is the evidence that He included same-sex marriage in the definition? No religion I know of has ever claimed that to be the case. God has never commanded any segment of society to practice same-sex marriage.

Natural law can never sanction unnatural behavior

If on the other hand, man created it, then its form and scope can be put to debate and a vote. In short, the whole case for same-sex marriage lies in the belief that such a right is government's to grant.

The whole marriage debate is but the latest manifestation of the great debate that animated our Founding Fathers – the nature of man and whether we have inherent and natural rights from our Creator, or whether such rights can only be dispensed by government.

Because our Founding Fathers resoundingly answered that we are endowed by our Creator with inalienable rights including life, liberty, and the pursuit of happiness, the following questions are before us:

- Is the freedom of marriage between a man and a woman of the same eminence as the freedoms affirmed by the Bill of Rights?

- Does same-sex marriage rise to that caliber?

- Does natural law grant people the right to a same-sex marriage?

By a 61-30 margin in a split-sample test, Americans believe that the right to traditional marriage between a man and a woman is equivalent to such rights as freedom of speech, freedom of religion and freedom of the press, while the same question posed for same-sex marriage elicited only 39% agreement and 55% disagreement. The idea that the Madisons, Adamses, and Jeffersons of our fledgling republic would have added same-sex marriage to the Bill of Rights doesn't hold up.

Marriage

"Do you feel that marriage ..."

Should only be between one man and one woman	64%
Should be redefined to include any two people regardless of gender	33

As for the third question, it is obvious on its face: Natural law can never sanction unnatural behavior.

If we are to believe that man created marriage and is justified in extending its definition because there is no special relationship between the two genders, then what institutions and rights cannot be reasoned to come from man?

If, however, our basic freedoms were not given to us by government, why should we believe that marriage was? And if marriage was not given to us by government, by what logic are advocates of same-sex marriage justified in changing its definition?

Our Position

We Mormons believe without any doubt that God ordained marriage as part of His plan for His children, and He instituted it even before He placed man on the earth. It was not man's idea. God created gender and the institution of marriage and family, specifics of which the LDS Church proclaimed to the world in 1995:[67]

- Marriage between a man and a woman is ordained of God and is essential to God's eternal plan.

- The family is ordained of God and is central to the Creator's plan for the eternal destiny of His children.

- The divine plan of happiness enables family relationships to be perpetuated beyond the grave.

- Gender is an essential characteristic of individual pre-mortal, mortal, and eternal identity and purpose.

- All of us accepted God's plan by which His children could obtain a physical body and gain earthly experience to progress toward perfection and ultimately realize his or her divine destiny as an heir of eternal life.

- The sacred powers of procreation are to be employed only between man and woman, lawfully wedded as husband and wife.

Gender, marriage, and family are all part of the master plan presented to us before we came to this earth. It is so clear and simple that I wonder how those who believe in God can possibly imagine that He would leave the definition of marriage in the hands of fallible men.

Consider also these specifics:

- Marriage was designed to last forever. It pre-dates any earthly government. If you believe the Bible and check the sequence of events in the second and third chapters of Genesis, you will find that Adam and Eve were man and wife before they became subject to death.

- Marriage is a dual-purpose agreement for the benefit of the couple and for children. It was never intended to be a single-purpose agreement for the benefit of the man and woman alone. Feelings of love between two individuals cannot by themselves define the institution.

- That infertility may prevent the creation of new life by a couple is no justification for including same-sex couples into that master-plan agreement.

- Death, divorce, and other circumstances may prevent a family from being complete, but do not change the ideal and are not a basis to extend the definition of family to living arrangements that run counter to God's master plan.

We distinguish between our beliefs about same-sex marriage and our personal relationships with gays and lesbians. Although 21% of Americans say we are bigoted homophobes and 55% say we are anti-gay, our doctrine states unequivocally that homosexual behavior is not natural and is a misuse of God-given procreative powers, and further, that marriage between man and woman is not to be trifled with.

Behavior

"Do you approve or disapprove of homosexual behavior?"

Approve	28%
Disapprove	53
No opinion / Refused	20

Our efforts to protect traditional marriage and oppose same-sex marriage are not an expression of how we feel about individuals who have same-sex attractions. President Gordon B. Hinckley explained it this way:

People inquire about our position on those who consider themselves so-called gays and lesbians. My response is that we love them as sons and daughters of God. They may have certain inclinations which are powerful and which may be difficult to control. Most people have inclinations of one kind or another at various times. If they do not act upon these inclinations, then they can go forward as do all other members of the Church. If they violate the law of chastity and the moral standards of the Church, then they are subject to the disciplines of the Church, just as others are. ... We want to help these people, to strengthen them, to assist them with their problems and to help them with their difficulties.[68]

He also said:

There is no justification to redefine what marriage is. Such is not our right, and those who try will find themselves answerable to God. ... As I said from this pulpit one year ago, our hearts reach out to those who refer to themselves as gays and lesbians. We love and honor them as sons and daughters of God. They are welcome in the Church. It is expected, however, that they follow the same God-given rules of conduct that apply to everyone else, whether single or married.[69]

Love and compassion for people, but opposition to their actions.

LGBT Agenda

At this point, let me identify a related issue that will, in my opinion, become even more significant and divisive in the future than same-sex marriage is today. And given that Mormons, individually if not necessarily as a church, will be drawn into the debate, an explanation of our position and reasoning may be useful. Here are our concerns about the impact of this issue ... on children.

While the LGBT community advances love and equality as reasons for same-sex marriage, their deeper purposes[70] revealed themselves in California in 2008. Between May and November of that year, same-sex marriage was legal in that state, but no more than 18,000 couples, if that, took advantage of it. Even if all had been from California, that is less than 3% of the gay population in that state. Why so few? Because gays and lesbians do not want marriage for the sake of marriage as much as they want society's stamp of approval of their lifestyle so they can achieve two goals:

- Unfettered legal access to impressionable young minds, and

- Squelch religious ministers from preaching against homosexual behavior.

Instead of parents deciding when and how their children will be introduced to social issues and controversies, gay activists agitate for elementary school children to be taught about same-sex marriage and the gay lifestyle.

Their indoctrination campaigns are subtle. During the Proposition 8 campaign in California, the LGBT community insisted that legalizing same-sex marriage would not lead to children in elementary schools being taught about the gay lifestyle. Yet that is precisely what has happened, even though same-sex marriage lost at the ballot box. Gay and lesbian lobbying recently succeeded in making gay history part of the required curriculum in California public schools. It parades under the guise that it will protect kids from bullying, but such instruction obviously raises curiosity that is neither appropriate nor necessary for their age.

Why must five-year-olds be taught about LGBTs when they're still learning their ABCs?

Gay activists know well their goals and have not chosen their targets randomly. They know that K-3 students are vulnerable because the pre-frontal cortex, the brain's seat of judgment, is only partially developed at ages five through eight, and hasn't hit its second surge of growth that begins at age 11.[71] Place certain thoughts in those minds early and reap an advantage as the student grows up.

Surreptitious conditioning: coming soon to a school near you.

Same-sex marriage has become a major wedge issue in our society. The related issue – at what age and *from whom* children receive information about other behaviors in society – will become even more salient in the public square. Our position is simple and strong: Same-sex marriage undermines the institution of marriage and the family – how can a change in the definition of marriage do anything but? It also undermines the belief that our rights and freedoms come from God, and thus contributes to the power and growth of government.

Weak families and large government. Now *there's* a formula for success.

CHAPTER 17

"Mormons Are Racist"

To a boy with a hammer, everything looks like a nail. To an antagonist with a thesis, everything looks like evidence.

The LDS Church once had a policy of excluding African-Americans from holding the priesthood. I cannot defend it; I can only acknowledge it, attempt to place it in the context of American culture of the time, and tell you where we are today.

The three-fold explanation involves the difference between doctrine and policy:

1. Our canonized *doctrines* have never been racist.

2. A *policy* regarding blacks and the priesthood, however, was racist from the second half of the 19th century to 1978. In the racist waters in which all Americans swam in the 1800s and well into the 1900s, practices evolved in Mormonism that we would find unthinkable to allow today.

3. Since 1978, no racist policies exist.

I will later address the problem of individual racists, a number of whom under various definitions will be found in any organization. But, facts being what they are, having once excluded blacks from the priesthood, the church has a steeper hill to climb to convince the world of its true principles – principles that were very clear from its earliest days.

The Established Doctrine: 1829-1845

Just as Christ's apostles faced challenges spreading His message to a Rome-dominated world that practiced slavery,[72] so too the re-established church in the 1830s in America.

Here are the principles God gave this fledgling church with the publication of the Book of Mormon in 1829 and in subsequent revelations to Joseph Smith, precisely during this period of pre-Civil War contention.[73]

- "Therefore, it is not right that any man should be in bondage one to another."

- "And there was a strict command throughout all the churches that there should be no persecutions among them, that there should be an equality among all men."

- "... all men are privileged the one like unto the other, and none are forbidden."

- "And again I say unto you, let every man esteem his brother as himself."

- "I say unto you, be one; and if ye are not one ye are not mine."

- "And let every man deal honestly, and be alike among this people, and receive alike, that ye may be one, even as I have commanded you."

- "For if ye are not equal in earthly things ye cannot be equal in obtaining heavenly things."

- "… I am no respecter of persons."

As for the priesthood itself, one of our scriptures states plainly:

> And now this calling and commandment give I unto you concerning *all men* – that as many as shall come … embracing this calling and commandment, shall be ordained and sent forth to preach the everlasting gospel among the nations….[74] (Emphasis added.)

There was and is no doubt what the ideal status of men one to another should be. The priesthood has always been destined for every man who is able and worthy – regardless of race – to preach Christ's doctrine.

When Mormons were driven out of Ohio in the 1830s and began settling in Missouri, it would have been easy for our people to go along with their neighbors in that slave state. They didn't, for all of the reasons in the above quotes. Fear that the growing Mormon population would flip the state into the free-state column was a major reason Governor Lilburn Boggs issued the infamous "Extermination Order" that all Mormons were to be killed or driven out of Missouri.[75]

Persecution intensified and no help came from either state or federal government. President Martin Van Buren told Joseph Smith in 1839, "If I take up with you, I will lose the vote of Missouri."[76] Boggs and Van Buren – profiles in courage.

The Mormons driven from Missouri settled in Illinois and built a city on the banks of the Mississippi called Nauvoo, larger than Chicago at the time, but the Missouri experience threatened to repeat. To bring the plight of this budding church to the attention of all Americans, Joseph Smith declared his candidacy for President of the United States.

He ran on a religious freedom and anti-slavery platform.

Cultural Influence: 1845-1978

Even as church practice drifted from doctrine about blacks and the priesthood, membership as a matter of policy has never been withheld from any person because of race or ethnicity. Any person eight years of age and over who believes that the LDS Church is the re-established original Christian church, and is willing to live God's commandments, is welcomed into membership through baptism.

It is also policy that we do not organize congregations for blacks and separate ones for whites, as certain other denominations do. Our congregations (we call them wards) are organized geographically, the boundaries being drawn to encompass 300 to 600 members. Whatever races found among our members within those defined neighborhoods or communities meet together.

Demographics such as income and education might be considered in drawing ward boundaries, but only to *assemble* diversity, not avoid it. Our policy is that people of all backgrounds should mix together as a ward family so that all may be strengthened through serving one another, and we never organize members by level of tithing contribution, or any other such criteria. No purchasing of pews allowed.

Except for those who do not speak the language of a host country, our congregations are not segregated. Such members by their choice may attend worship services conducted in whatever language they feel most comfortable.

That being said, culture and perhaps personal preferences began to influence church practices in the 1850s when racism was commonplace in America. Several black members were given the priesthood during Joseph Smith's lifetime in accordance with the doctrines cited above, but this practice dwindled after the church migrated to the Great Salt Lake Valley in 1847, and at least one black high priest was not allowed to participate in temple worship.

One explanation is that Brigham Young was reacting to a black Mormon's attempt to seduce women into a polygamist practice. Another is that it was an accommodation to new Mormon converts from southern states who brought their slaves with them to Utah (census in 1860: 59 blacks, 29 of whom were slaves). Additional explanations focus on a post-Civil War concern about interracial marriage that remained an issue throughout America into the 1950s.

Some Mormons justified the exclusionary practice by claiming that those of African descent come from the lineage of Cain who was cursed with a mark, and/or that they were not as valiant as others during the war in heaven, fence-sitters as it were. Both theories have been discredited and few Mormons subscribe to them.

Whatever ideas crept into church administration, the scriptures never changed; there was never a doctrine that blacks should be excluded from the priesthood. The struggle was overcoming the cultural biases of the time so that practice and doctrine would be one.

Our actions mirrored the nation when we should have been ahead of it, as we were with women's suffrage, when Mormon-dominated Utah granted women the vote 50 years before all women in the nation were enfranchised.[77]

Back on Track: 1978

Much has been written on the cultural period in LDS history as our people struggled to reconcile policy, practice, and ideal principles, especially as America's racial attitudes began to change, and this chapter cannot cover all the this-apostle-that-apostle debates on the matter. But it was never doctrine that certain races would never hold the priesthood. It was always understood that the right of all worthy men to be given the priesthood was never a matter of *if*, only a matter of *when*.

The Lord lets people struggle with problems until a unity of hearts is achieved

As proposals were advanced and positions argued, two patterns became clear:

- Discussions of strongly held viewpoints are often necessary before unity of hearts can be achieved.

- The Lord lets people struggle with problems before He provides the answer that gets things back on track.

For example, Joseph Smith had to ask questions about baptism before the Lord sent John the Baptist in person to restore the authority to perform them. Similarly, early members in the 1830s had to debate the use of tobacco before the Lord revealed what we call the Word of Wisdom forbidding its use.

In such cases, it takes time for people to recognize that something may be out of whack, for cultural attitudes to change, and for time to winnow the adherents of a point of view. United States racial policies shifted markedly in 1954 and again in 1964-65.[78] Ours shifted in the 1970s.

Unity of policy and doctrine was finally achieved and announced on June 8, 1978, key excerpts from the official Church Declaration stating:

> As we have witnessed the expansion of the work of the Lord over the earth, we have been grateful that people of many nations have responded to the message of the restored gospel, and have joined the Church in ever-increasing numbers. This, in turn, has inspired us with a desire to extend to every worthy member of the Church all of the privileges and blessings which the gospel affords. ...
>
> [The Lord] has heard our prayers, and by revelation has confirmed that the long-promised day has come when every faithful, worthy man in the Church may receive the holy priesthood, with power to exercise its divine authority, and enjoy with his loved ones every blessing that flows therefrom, including the blessings of the temple. Accordingly, all worthy male members of the Church may be ordained to the priesthood without regard for race or color.[79]

Note the sequence: the *expansion* of the work *inspired* the leaders of the church with a *desire*. Followers of the Lord have always been commanded to be unified and to be one. So when events on the ground, such as our fast growth, triggered the recognition that culture cannot override long-established doctrine, and once all of the leaders came to a unity of minds, the green light was given and the church moved forward. The Lord was the gatekeeper, not the roadblock. Since then, membership in the church has more than tripled.

I heard about it that day on a radio newscast and I wept tears of joy.

This revelation, however, was more than permission to ordain worthy blacks to the priesthood. It reaffirmed the original doctrines given in the early days of the church, unleashed a "flood of intelligence and light,"[80] and caused previous defenders of the policy to update their opinions and disavow previous statements on the matter.[81]

Gordon B. Hinckley, an apostle in 1978 and later president of the church, said in 2006:

> We all rejoiced in the 1978 revelation given President Kimball. I was there in the temple at the time that that happened. There was no doubt in my mind or in the minds of my associates that what was revealed was the mind and the will of the Lord.[82]

As one prominent black member, Darius Gray, has observed, "It took revelation by God to set right something that had gotten somehow misplaced."

Individual Members

That policy having been put to rest, what about the members?

Darius Gray nailed it when he said, "Is there racism in the church? Yes, because we are a cross-section of the United States, of the people here. Now, is the Church of Jesus Christ of Latter-day Saints racist? No, never has been. But some of those people within the church have those tendencies. You have to separate the two."[84]

Image Traits
Mormons are racist:
Yes — 15%
No — 73
No opinion — 12

It is no surprise, in a church that functions among the cultures of over 130 countries, that we would have racist Neanderthals at one end of the scale and saints without a racist bone in their body-houses at the other, with most falling somewhere in between. Unfortunately, the racists we do have may be particularly stubborn because they feel there is scriptural justification (a problematic interpretation of the story of Cain) for denying blacks the priesthood.

But the vast majority of members do not deserve to be labeled by an antagonist with an agenda. Racism, in my opinion, is a scaled attitude and not a binary you-are-or-you-aren't variable. Those who have been conditioned to believe that yesterday's mistakes are today's racism will even judge a Mormon on the low end of this scale as evidence that Latter-day Saints are racist. Their boy-with-a-hammer syndrome is no more becoming of them than pockets of racism are of us.

The real question on which we should be judged is: What are we doing about whatever level of individual member racism may exist?

Former President Gordon B. Hinckley bluntly directed the men in the church:

> There is no basis for racial hatred among the priesthood of this Church. If any within the sound of my voice is inclined to indulge in this, then let him go before the Lord and ask for forgiveness and be no more involved in such.[85]

The standards are in place, the doctrine is clear, and there is no question what the relationship between people should be. I for one will not be satisfied until the behavior of every member conforms to our doctrine that our people should be "of one heart and one mind." A few old ideas must exit the stage, boots first.

As my good friend and expert on the issue Marvin Perkins put it, "Even though this issue is one of the biggest thorns in the side of The Church of Jesus Christ of Latter-day Saints, it is also one of the biggest opportunities for our growth as we go forth sharing the new understanding that we have and correcting the errors of our ways." [86]

The few are not the many, and yesterday is not today.

CHAPTER 18

"Mormons Help the Poor, But Only if They're Mormons"

How many churches keep tons of foodstuffs, clothes and medical supplies on pallets ready for quick loading onto cargo planes to be flown anywhere in the world when a disaster strikes?

And the inscription "For Mormons Only" will not be found on any of it.

Not to put too fine of a trumpet on it, but if the stats were gathered, I would wager that the per-capita amounts Mormons contribute to non-Mormon poor would compete favorably with the contributions from any other religion to those not on their rolls. In 2008, for example, the church responded to 124 disasters in 48 countries, and since 1985, such help has been given to 23 million people in 163 nations. We do not have 23 million members.

Other efforts include building clean water services in third-world countries that provide access to clean water (for four million people in Africa alone where our numbers are fewer than 400,000), pro-

> ## Image Traits
>
> Mormons are willing to share with the
> needy no matter their religion.
>
> | | |
> |---|---|
> | Yes | 66% |
> | No | 18 |
> | Don't know | 17 |

viding thousands of wheelchairs, inoculating millions of children against diseases, and providing 300 job development and placement centers throughout the world.

Mormons are aggressively, visibly involved in helping those in need around the world, Mormons or not. That's the easy part. The problem religions and governments have faced since the invention of hunger is how to help the less fortunate avoid dependency, move beyond today's needs, and achieve ongoing self-sufficiency.

Anyone can give a man a fish; teaching a man to fish is another matter.

The LDS Welfare Plan: Empower, Not Entitle

In the middle of the Depression, our church created a welfare plan to assist the poor:

> Our primary purpose was to set up, insofar as possible, a system under which the curse of idleness would be done away with, the evils of the dole abolished, and independence, industry, thrift, and self-respect be once more established amongst our people. The aim of the Church is to help the people to help themselves. Work is to be re-enthroned as the ruling principle of the lives of our Church membership.[87]

Note the focus on building character: work, independence, industry, thrift, and self-respect. We have discovered that once those qualities are re-established, filling tummies is a natural result.

In comparison, governments rarely talk about such traits. Their idea is to give people money and food stamps, and hope the problem will somehow be eased. Such an attitude only makes it worse. For example, self-sustaining people often are educated and own homes, but subsidizing education and home ownership will not produce self-sustaining people. That requires training of character.[88]

One indicator of this retrogression is the name used to describe assistance. It was first called the dole, a word that carried a stigma, as in "evils of." At least with the first government assistance programs, people recognized that being on the dole should, for purposes of self-respect, be of short duration.

That changed. The dole soon became known as welfare, then assistance, and then ... *entitlement.*

Clever word, that. The root suggests an attainment of worth. It could be an earned or bestowed rank or office, or a possession, such as holding title to an estate or property. Either way, a title is a plus; it carries the connotation of a *deserved privilege.*

The person who receives private assistance is more likely to pass it forward

---

In today's usage, the positive word entitlement invites the non-needy to participate in upwards of 100 federal assistance programs in the United States because it not only eliminates stigma, it conveys an honorable attainment should the person conform to the formula for the handout. So practiced, it brings a false sense of being worthy.

Let me be clear: I am not referring to those who are disabled, lacking in marketable skills through no fault of their own, or otherwise genuinely disadvantaged. Church and society must, and do, render assistance. Rather, I am faulting an attitude found too often among America's healthy, marketable, and capable – the attitude of entitlement.

Such behavior runs contrary to what our church stands for. We believe ...

- People should be anxiously engaged in helping others, and bearing one another's burdens.

- God created a planet of plenty and there is enough for all if we responsibly manage resources.

- That any person having abundance must share a portion with the poor and needy.

- That people should work to the best of their ability for any assistance they receive.

- The idler should not eat the bread of the laborer.

- The first line of defense against need is the individual himself, followed by his family, and then the church.

The aim of church welfare is to help the people to help themselves – to support life, not a lifestyle.

Advantages Over Government Programs

Government-run charity satisfies today's hunger, but fails to build tomorrow's independence. When people receive help from government, whom do they approach, look in the eye and say, "Thank you!" in a heartfelt way? And further, from whom do they receive direction and support for taking the important next steps to become self-sufficient, to evolve from one in need to someone who can not only care for his own needs but help others as well?

Helping the Poor

In a 2010 Lawrence Research national survey, respondents were asked to imagine that their neighbor told them that he and his family did not have enough food to eat, and were then asked their level of agreement with the following statements:

I have a moral obligation to help him.	91%
Government has a duty to provide food for him.	58%
He has the right to demand that government help him.	39%
Government has the right to increase my taxes so that he can be helped.	41%
Government should increase my taxes so it can help him.	29%

With no personal interaction, recipients in time come to view the charity as a right and (that word again) entitlement. The administrators of government funds, however compassionate they personally may be, are mere conduits applying unbending formulas with little latitude for judgment of unique circumstances. Any feelings of gratitude that once may have impelled a pass-it-forward attitude are squashed.

Compare that to a person who is being helped by a welfare program that relies on voluntary contributions rather than forced taxation. The giver who recognizes that all he possesses comes from God does not feel superior to the recipient. The recipient so blessed by the charity feels an obligation to respond in kind, to become self-reliant, and that when he is blessed with possessions, to share them with others. The character of both improves.

In the LDS Church system, we ask all members to go without food for two meals on the first Sunday of each month and to contribute the cost of those two meals to help the poor. It doesn't take anything out of the family budget, and a look in the national mirror would suggest that Americans could survive quite nicely forgoing two meals a month.

Because the recipient knows that the people he sees in church each Sunday went hungry to help the poor, he will feel more responsibility to use the charity wisely. Further, he can say thanks to a flesh-and-blood person – the bishop who is guiding his growth and represents all the givers. That bishop also taps resources to assist with educational counseling, employment opportunities, and networking. Personal bonds are established, gratitude is not a one-off thing, and sweet, character-building experiences are the result.

I know. It happened to my family when I was 13 and the oldest of six children, and my father was hospitalized for 18 months with a crippling disease.

I have seen the church's welfare program from all three sides – as a recipient, as a contributor, and as a bishop charged with actively seeking out the poor and deciding how best to help them.

The program works because gratitude together with personal counseling becomes an empowering mechanism that no public program can match.

Going hungry to help the hungry is truly sharing the burden.

CHAPTER 19

"Mormons Treat Women as Second-Class Citizens"

L ike any church, we have our "me Tarzan you Jane" types. But there is no church policy that justifies such condescension, and we would applaud if the Janes would knock the Tarzans off their swinging vines.

Again we go back to the beginning. There are two genders, there is a master plan, there is marriage, and there is the family unit. In other words, there is an organization.

I think it is fairly well accepted that for any organization to function, someone must preside, someone must lead, and someone must be ultimately accountable at the top. Leaders and followers are divisions of labor, not class distinctions. And that applies whether the organization is a business, a church, or a family.

The issue is whether the leader of a family leads as God intends.

Policy – The Church

The main reason critics say we view women as second-class citizens is because we do not ordain them to the priesthood. There is much more substance to the discussion of the roles of men and women, however, than what relates to the priesthood.

Let me explain the organization. We believe the head of the church is Jesus Christ Himself. Serving at His direct appointment is the First Presidency consisting of the President of the Church, whom we consider the Lord's prophet, and two counselors. Under them comes the Quorum of the Twelve Apostles who are exactly that – apostles of the Lord Jesus Christ, same number and same function as in New Testament times.

The top-down hierarchy continues with eight quorums of the Seventy divided into 26 geographic areas of the world, 2900 stake presidents (think diocese) and then 29,000 bishops and branch presidents who preside at the local level.

Now the rub for some women: all of these officers are men – every single one of them. Proves first-class and second-class citizenship, right?

Well, only if you believe that holding the priesthood is a status symbol to be sought, that a division of labor means inequality, and that the Lord didn't mean to choose all men as His apostles and line officers in the first place.

Image Traits

Among Mormons ...

Women are second-class citizens

Yes	36%
No	45
No opinion	19

What is often overlooked is that the priesthood can never be used for oneself. A priesthood holder cannot place his hands on his own head and give himself a blessing. The priesthood power can only be used to bless the lives of others. It was never intended to be a status symbol.

Further, the assumption has crept into society that a woman is less than complete unless she can do everything a man can do. (The reverse might just as well be pondered, by the way.) Because society gets hung up over who presides, women themselves contribute much to the idea that they have second-class status. It surely hasn't been men telling them they must be able to do all things men can do. It's *women* setting a *male* bar for other *women* – telling Jane to ape Tarzan, so to speak.

If only we would realize that one can preside yet both can be equal. Equality is not sameness.

That said, when asked about the role for women in leadership positions and prominent activities, we explain that women preside over and lead three key organizations in the church: the Relief Society, one of the oldest and largest women's organizations in the world; the Young Women organization that teaches girls 12-18; and the Primary organization that instructs all children under 12 years of age. We also point out that women give sermons and prayers in our worship services, and also officiate in certain temple ordinances.

But more important here than any leadership or responsibilities is to recognize two patterns from long ago and far away.

First, it was Eve, not Adam, who first got the big picture. Some religions blame Eve for eating the forbidden fruit and claim that, but for her, we would all be living in a paradise called the Garden of Eden.

We believe that is incorrect. Adam and Eve at that time were not yet mortal – that is, they were not yet subject to death. As such, they could not have children until they were. Adam was thinking linearly when told not to eat the forbidden fruit ("gotta keep the commandments, gotta keep the commandments"), while Eve thought holistically and realized they had to eat the forbidden fruit so a higher commandment – to become mortal and multiply and replenish the earth – could be fulfilled.

Eve grasped the big picture first

Mormons are one of few religions that do not condemn Eve for her act. Rather, we praise her. She was not a second-class citizen then and neither are her daughters today.

Second, no heavenly messenger in Judeo-Christian history has ever been a woman, but this absence of participation cannot possibly indicate second-class citizenship in those realms of glory above. Knowing that we have heavenly parents, can any of us believe our Mother in heaven plays an inferior role to the Father? Doesn't compute.

As I have watched my wife, my mother, six aunts, five sisters and three daughters, I can state unequivocally that women live on a higher spiritual plane and communicate more easily with God than do men.

Maybe men were given the priesthood so they could catch up.

Policy – The Family

The roles of men and women are clearly detailed in the church's proclamation on the family:

By divine design, fathers are to preside over their families in love and righteousness and are responsible to provide the necessities of life and protection for their families. Mothers are primarily responsible for the nurture of their children. In these sacred responsibilities, fathers and mothers are obligated to help one another as equal partners.[89]

Note the division of labor and especially the "equal partners."

The proclamation then states emphatically:

We warn that individuals who violate covenants of chastity, who abuse spouse or offspring, or who fail to fulfill family responsibilities will one day stand accountable before God.

The church isn't kidding about Tarzan.

Building a house takes many specialties – designer, framer, carpenter, plumber, electrician, roofer, painter, and so on. The same thing applies to building a family, but the many specialties have to be embodied in only two people. Without stereotyping too much, the man is the external force – providing, protecting, leading – while the woman is the internal force – caring, nurturing, educating. Each brings special traits to the task.

In their most basic roles, the man as the giver of life and woman as the producer of life, division of labor has never meant inequality. Neither is more important than the other and neither person can fulfill both roles, nor can either fulfill his or her roles without the other. When gender was created, so was division of labor. And such assignments in no way presage a division of glory, attainment, or reward.

These roles in no way suggest that God views one gender as inferior to the other.

Behavior

Which brings us to where we started.

I maintain that a neutral sociologist would find that the LDS Church contains no greater percentage of Tarzans, plus or minus, than other churches. And where there are problems, much can be traced to not understanding the difference between a leader and a boss.

In corporations, the presiding officer may be both leader and boss, but not in the church or the family. Neither the man nor the woman is the boss. The man presides and is designated the accountable leader, but no woman has a duty to follow a husband who does not follow God. The system works only as the husband obeys God and thus *wins* his wife's willingness to follow him.

Unfortunately, this principle is ignored by feminists who want to wear the pants and by Tarzans who think their maleness makes them the unquestioned power. They're both hung up on *boss* – which connotes control and force – when they should be focused on *leader*, which connotes love, persuasion, and example. A compromise between pant-nappers and vine-swingers should not be difficult if both would erase the boss notion from their thinking.

In the classic TV series *The Honeymooners*, Jackie Gleason as Ralph Cramden is reading the riot act to his wife, Alice.

> Ralph: "I'm the boss, Alice. *I'm* the boss. You got that? You got that? You're nothing, Alice. I'm the boss and you're nothing."

> Alice: "I got it, Ralph. You're the boss over nothing."

To hold the priesthood is to preside. The father presides with love in the home, and in counsel with his wife they together make family decisions as both obey the commandments of God. There is no place for a boss.

But if a man ever uses his priesthood as an excuse to "exercise control or dominion or compulsion upon the souls of the children of men, in any degree of unrighteousness," it is our doctrine that it's goodbye to the priesthood – the right to preside – of that man.[90]

When that happens, his wife retains the first-class status she has always possessed and the husband loses his role as the leader.

He truly becomes the boss over nothing.

CHAPTER 20

"Mormon Leaders Control Every Facet of a Mormon's Life"

Funny how being organized, involved, and motivated can be so misinterpreted.

In a classic *Peanuts* cartoon, Lucy asks Charlie Brown and Linus what they see as they look at cloud formations. Linus sees a map of British Honduras, a profile of Thomas Eakins, and an impression of the stoning of Stephen, with the Apostle Paul standing to the side. Charlie Brown sees a duckie and a horsie.

Conditioned perspective.

Whenever the church mobilizes its members to clean up after a hurricane, look for a lost child, walk precincts for a moral ballot issue, or join a community betterment project, not a few members have been asked, "How do you Mormons do it?"

Usually we mumble something about having wonderful members who are motivated to help others, make communities a better place to live, and so on.

Those observations are true, but we do not have a corner on such people. They are to be found in all denominations.

So how can we put 25,000 members in California knocking on doors with but a week's notice, organize a search party of hundreds within a matter of minutes, organize hundreds of clean-up crews from eight or ten neighboring states to travel to the Gulf Coast to help people, both ours and those of other faiths, clear hurricane debris and rebuild their lives?

It's possible because of our beliefs and our commitment to Christian service, but also because of three sociological characteristics – vertical, geographic, and unpaid – that, to my knowledge, no other denomination fully matches.

Vertical

We are a top-down religion for doctrine, for conveying authority, and for church policies as the Lord reveals His will to the prophet who then counsels us accordingly.

But we are both a vertical and horizontal organization when it comes to putting our beliefs into practice at the local level. I saw this happen when a young man became lost in the Santa Cruz, California mountains after a church-sponsored day-trip. After a fruitless search, the sheriff's department was notified and they told my bishop to recruit as many people as possible to begin a search at daybreak. The call went out at 11:00 that night, and by 6:00 the next morning an unbelievable horde was available for deputy sheriffs to instruct and take into the woods. Within an hour the young man was found, cold but not bad off for wear.

The key was that the bishop did not have to spend time calling his counterparts in neighboring wards. All it took was a phone call to the stake president (the bishop's ecclesiastical superior) and then he called his counselors who then called down the line to bishops, to other ward leaders and then horizontally, members to members. Nobody had to call more than five people and hundreds showed up. As we prepared to return to our homes, the deputies told us, "We have never seen a bigger turnout of volunteers in a faster time than from you Mormons."

The church tries to strike a balance between vertical direction and individual creativity. If an individual has a problem, he is expected to do all he can to solve it. If it is beyond his means and skills, the immediate family and then the extended family are the next sources of assistance. If still more help is needed, the bishop steps in with the resources of the ward.

For larger community or state problems, such as natural or economic disasters, resources and manpower are mobilized from as many wards and stakes as needed. The guiding principle is that a problem is best solved at the level closest to the problem. Those activities are figured out in ward, stake, or area councils.

Top-to-bottom verticality plays a role mainly to guarantee that doctrine, policies, and ordinances are uniformly adhered to. Our top leaders give counsel at general and local meetings to encourage us to exercise agency, take responsibility for our actions, and do many good things on our own initiative.

But to say that they want to control our lives (as 57% of Americans imagine) or that we are brainwashed (33%) is nonsense.

Geographic

Whatever address members have anywhere in the world, they will know what meetinghouse they should go to for worship services. They will belong to that specific congregation and be listed on its roll. They will become part of that ward family.

Few religions draw congregational lines as we do. Those of other faiths are usually free to choose which church within their denomination they wish to attend. All denominations that pay their ministers must engage in marketing efforts to remain financially stable, and even preachers from the same religion may find themselves in competition with each other. Attendance waxes and wanes depending on the quality of the preaching and assorted blandishments.

This competition affects their volunteer efforts. Not a few ministers hesitate to ask their parishioners to join hands with those of other faiths, or even those within their same denomination, in a common volunteer cause because they're afraid that someone might say, "You ought to come visit our church."

Preachers are prickly about poachers when their paychecks depend upon putting parishioners in the pews.

By comparison, you will never hear of an LDS bishop marketing his worship services to members of a neighboring ward. It simply does not happen.

Not only do we save time and money by eliminating intra-church competition, if a disaster strikes, each bishop knows who the members are in the affected area and which members are closest to provide assistance.

Unpaid

In a motion to begin the 1787 Constitutional Convention sessions with prayer, Benjamin Franklin said, "I have lived, sir, a long time; and the longer I live, the more convincing proofs I see of this truth, that God governs in the affairs of men. And if a sparrow cannot fall to the ground without His notice, is it probable that an empire can rise without His aid?"

The motion died for lack of funds to pay a minister to offer the prayers.[91]

What does this say about the "business" of religion? After all that the colonists had sacrificed to win our freedom, no man of the cloth would step forward and ask God's blessings on those critical proceedings without being paid?

We preach for free what the Savior gave us for free

The big sociological difference between the LDS Church and other denominations is that none of our local leaders are paid. We preach for free what the Savior gave us for free. Not a religious franchisee among us.

Ask a Mormon bishop what his occupation is and you may hear engineer, farmer, truck driver, doctor, teacher, mechanic, attorney, salesman, and many others, but you will never hear the word bishop.

Of course, every major organization needs full-time leaders and staff at the top, but paying ministers at the local level? Where did that idea come from? Did Peter sit down one day and ask himself, "What job could I invent so I could have fine clothes, the admiration of the community, and not smell like fish?"

No, the work of the ministry in New Testament days was performed by unpaid labor. And so the question today: Why not split up the work of ministering to members' needs *among the members themselves,* give everyone an occasional opportunity to preach the Sunday sermon, and have everyone get a weekday job?

That's the way we do it. Every member, for example, is assigned a home teacher who is asked to visit once a month and assist as needs arise. Every child from age three on up learns how to give a talk in front of others. And beginning at age 12, all members are given the opportunity – usually once or twice a year – to address the congregation in our main worship service called a sacrament meeting.

No stake president, no bishop, and no other leaders in our local congregations make a penny from their church assignments.

The website Payscale.com estimates the average annual pay for ministers in the United States is around $44,000. If these salaries were applied to the LDS bishops and branch presidents in the approximately 14,000 wards and branches in America, it would mean $620 million would be spent just to put rice and beans on their tables and roofs over their families' heads.

The outlay would not stop at bishops. Counselors, youth leaders, heads of auxiliaries, and even organists and choristers and gardeners, jobs that are common on many denominations' payrolls, would expect a share. Assuming we limited salaries to only five key people in each ward and paid them the average minister's salary, we would shovel out over *three billion* dollars per year in clergy pay in the United States alone, probably around *five billion* a year worldwide.

Five billion dollars a year pays for a lot of meetinghouses, temples, missionary work, publications, humanitarian outreach, and support for the poor.

Our 180-year tradition of everyone having a calling – everyone assigned to do a little something (the most time-consuming callings are for specified periods, five years for a bishop, for example) – has fostered a unique Mormon work ethic. We are participants, not spectators.

Let me repeat that. Because we are *participating* members instead of pew potatoes, when volunteers are needed, leaders need only describe the goal and give us a map. We do not need to be convinced that volunteerism is good; it's how we're built.

Having an unpaid clergy is a tremendous blessing. Dividing up the work helps members grow and take on positions of responsibility, which in turn has accelerated the growth of the church.

An Illinois legislator once asked Joseph Smith how he was able to govern so many people and preserve such perfect order. Joseph replied, "I teach them correct principles, and they govern themselves."[92]

We are more than a Sunday religion. We are a freely chosen way of life.

CHAPTER 21

"Mormons Think They Are Better Than Other People"

Although 25% have that impression, that statement is not correct. But we do believe that the nation that headquarters the LDS Church is the most blessed nation on earth.

We believe the re-establishment in 1830 of the original Christian church was the culmination of many factors beginning with the signing of the Magna Carta in 1215 and moving successively into the Renaissance as conditioner, the Reformation as forerunner, the settling of America by seekers of religious freedom, and the creation of the Constitution of the United States as the foundation.

We believe these events were instigated and guided by the hand of God so that America could become the base of operations for spreading the message of Jesus Christ throughout the world prior to His Second Coming.

The religious freedom necessary to accommodate this restoration or re-establishment could not have happened under any other system of government or any other nation at the time, which is why many

American Mormons are unabashedly patriotic and make no wimp-out excuses for being so.

A Divinely Inspired Constitution

Because of specific revelations on the matter, Mormons believe that the U.S. Constitution was divinely inspired, and that the events leading to it were directly guided by God:

> **The Founders:** It is statistically highly improbable that the great collection of talent, wisdom, and leadership of our Founding Fathers could randomly exist in any pool of three million people. God selected certain spirits to be born at just the right time and in just the right locations to pull off victory in the Revolutionary War and to create the Constitution.

Mormons believe the founding of the United States was guided by God

---

> **The Principles:** The Constitution is an amazing collection of immutable truths and principles that guide the exercise and control of power, the scope of government, and the role of the individual in polity. It recognizes the individual as no other founding documents ever have, as possessors of inherent rights and self-responsible agents to act for themselves, with minimal interference from power seekers. No longer were people to be subjects to a sovereign monarch under the imbecilic concept of divine right of kings, but they were to be sovereigns themselves – sovereigns over their government (though at times today one might wonder).

The Constitution

In my 2011 study, people were asked which of two statements comes closer to their own opinion about the United States Constitution:

It is an inspired document that contains correct principles that still apply today	83%
It is an outdated document and no longer applies to the modern world	13

In the 2010 study, the choices were phrased this way:

The Constitution contains time-honored principles and should be interpreted according to the Founding Fathers' original intent	58%
The Constitution is a living document and should be interpreted according to today's conditions and challenges	39

Advantage to the originalists, but the battle continues.

The Example: We believe that God has specifically stated that the U.S. Constitution was established for the rights and protection of *all* people, not only Americans. Because of the just principles it contains, it was destined to become, and indeed has become, the light of freedom for the world. Almost every country has copied all or part of the U.S. Constitution. (Whether the principles are being honored in practice is another matter. Recent studies show that a majority of nations pay homage to the model, but 70% of the world's population live in countries with substantial regulatory hindrances or no de facto religious freedom at all.)[93]

There was no doubt in the minds of the Founding Fathers as to where the inspiration for this document came from or for what purposes. The religious underpinnings of this document were well known to them:

> **John Adams:** "Our Constitution was made only for a moral and religious people. It is wholly inadequate to the government of any other."[94]

> **George Washington:** "The success, which has hitherto attended our united efforts, we owe to the gracious interposition of Heaven, and to that interposition let us gratefully ascribe the praise of victory, and the blessings of peace."[95]

> **Alexander Hamilton:** "For my own part, I sincerely esteem it a system, which without the finger of God, never could have been suggested and agreed upon by such a diversity of interest." [96]

> **James Madison:** "It is impossible for the man of pious reflection not to perceive in it a finger of that Almighty hand which has been so frequently and signally extended to our relief in the critical stages of the revolution."[97]

A Promised Land

Jesus Christ, the Creator of this earth under the direction of the Father, caused that a chosen land would be protected by geography to maximize its ability to remain free from tyrants. We believe this continent has always been a designated promised land, a pristine religious refuge for those who truly seek to worship God according to the dictates of their conscience.

The promise of this land is stated clearly in the Book of Mormon:

> Behold, this is a choice land, and whatsoever nation shall possess it shall be free from bondage, and from captivity, and from all other nations under heaven, if they will but serve the God of the land, who is Jesus Christ....[98]

Further, this LDS book of scripture states numerous times that if the possessors of this land will keep the commandments of God, they will prosper. If they do not, they will be cut off from His presence.

But, you ask, what about the Jews in America who don't believe in Jesus Christ?

Well, here's the deal: if they will worship the God of Abraham, Isaac, and Jacob, we'll call it close enough.

An Exceptional Nation Because God Said So

No one who understands American history can say with a straight face that America is no more exceptional than any other nation. Make no mistake: no well-grounded Mormon would ever agree with that position. And three out of four Americans agree. In our 2011 study we asked whether people believe ...

America is an exceptional nation	76%
Or	
A nation that is more or less like any other	20

Only one in five believes the idea emanating from some leaders that America is no more exceptional than any other nation, that it is more or less like any other.

Mormons believe America is exceptional because …

- Its founding was guided by God and its Constitution was inspired of God.

- It was the first country to establish the people as the sovereign over government.

- It broke from the stifling traditions of royalty and provided a home for the restless doers (the jibe that America is full of ADHDs is not far off) who chafed under the aristocratic systems in the countries of their birth.

- It allows success through hard work and by following correct principles, and by so doing has become the most productive nation in history.

- Its freedoms and opportunities have released the greatest creative forces – entrepreneurs, inventors, manufacturers, technologists, and every other endeavor – the world has seen.

- It has fought for, liberated, and protected the freedom of people in numerous countries.

- It has religious freedom – the most significant and important freedom of all.

- Its success is necessary to prepare people for the Second Coming of Christ.

And America is especially exceptional for one simple reason: God blessed it to be a stable base of operations so the re-established church could become a world-wide church and bless the lives of people in all nations.

CHAPTER 22

"Mormons Think Civilization Hinges On Freedom of Religion"

Guilty as charged.

Most of the criticisms we have examined in this book come from competing Christian denominations. This one, however, is aimed not only at Mormons, but many other religions as well. It comes from secularists – those who mock the supposedly archaic values of what they call "flyover country," reject the idea of absolute truths, and think that man's mind is the highest power in the universe.

We respectfully disagree. We believe freedom of religion is much more important than intellectual elites say it is. It is a God-given immutable principle that is the linchpin of all other freedoms and the key to prosperity.

America will always have enemies. There will be those who covet this productive land and would harness its citizens to their own ideologies if they could. There will be the jealous who have an ingrained hostility toward any group that is successful, prosperous, and independent, and would like to see America take it in the chops.

But the more insidious will be those who undermine religious freedom while claiming that they are protecting citizens from hate speech and discrimination, even violence. In their book *The Price of Freedom Denied*, Brian J. Grim and Roger Finke demonstrate with data from nearly 200 countries, however, that "restricting religious freedom is associated with higher levels of violent persecution."[99]

In the arguments we will likely hear come election seasons ahead, remember that a politician's promise to protect the freedom of *worship* is not the same as protecting the freedom of *religion*. Not by a long shot.

No Church of America

We Mormons strongly believe in the God-given religious freedoms affirmed in the First Amendment to the U.S. Constitution and will do all we can to protect them – namely that "Congress shall make no law respecting an establishment of religion, or prohibiting the free exercise thereof."

Picture the mindset in Philadelphia in 1787 when those words were written. Victorious revolutionaries were hammering out the fundamental guidelines by which their new nation would operate and up comes the question of religion. Memories of the state-controlled religions of Europe were fresh – Church of England, Church of Sweden, Church of Norway, or Church of Fill-In-The-Blank telling people how they must worship, and collecting taxes for their trouble. Few wanted government establishing a state-sanctioned religion here, unless, of course, their own denomination would get both miter and gavel. But because of America's diversity of religions and its unique de facto pluralism, no one was willing to take a chance on missing the jackpot, so better to deny government sponsorship to all.

And so it was. No Church of America. No state-established church favoring with political power one theology over another. No mixing of ecclesiastical and political authority.

Without religious teachings, America could not employ enough police to guarantee compliance with the law

---

Then, to make sure of government neutrality, the second clause regarding religion stipulated that Congress shall make no law prohibiting the free exercise thereof.

Should have been clear: no state-established religion and keep the government's mitts off all religious activities.

Why Religion Deserves Extra Protections

Religion is the first freedom mentioned in the Bill of Rights because our Founding Fathers recognized it as the glue that holds society together. In a speech at Chapman University in California in early 2011, Elder Dallin H. Oaks pointed out why religious teachings and religious organizations deserve special legal protection.[100] Synopsizing ...

> **Charity.** Charitable works originate most significantly from religious impulses and religious organizations. Our nation's incredible generosity manifests our common religious faith that all peoples are children of God. Religious beliefs instill patterns of altruistic behavior.

Morality. The great moral advances in Western society, such as the abolition of the slave trade and the Emancipation Proclamation, have been motivated by religious principles, not by secular ethics or coalitions who believed in moral relativism.

Honesty. For most of us, ideas of right and wrong are grounded in religious principles and teachings of religious leaders. The operation of modern technology in our economic system rests upon honesty.

Self-regulation. Our society is not held together just by law and its enforcement, but most importantly by voluntary obedience to the unenforceable and by widespread adherence to unwritten norms of righteous behavior, behaviors that would not exist save for religious teachings of right and wrong.

Religious Freedom

"The First Amendment addresses five freedoms. After I read them, please tell me which one you feel is most important." Then ... "If one of these freedoms is ever threatened, which one is it likely to be?"

	Most Important	Most Likely Threatened
Freedom of assembly	3%	9%
Freedom to petition government	9	12
Freedom of the press	3	11
Freedom of religion	31	33
Freedom of speech	47	28

Worth. Religious principles of human worth and dignity were instrumental in the origin of the Constitution, and only those principles in the hearts of our citizens can sustain that Constitution today.

He concludes: "I submit that religious values and political realities are so inter-linked in the origin and perpetuation of this nation that we cannot lose the influence of religions in our public life without seriously jeopardizing our freedoms."

Similar sentiments were spoken by President Calvin Coolidge in 1924:

Our government rests upon religions. It is from that source that we derive our reverence for truth and justice, for equality and liberality and for the rights of mankind. Unless the people believe in these principles they cannot believe in our government. There are only two main theories of government in the world. One rests on righteousness and the other on force. One appeals to reason, the other appeals to the sword. One is exemplified in a republic, the other is represented by a despotism.

The government of a country never gets ahead of the religions of a country. There is no way by which we can substitute the authority of law for the virtue of men. Of course we can help to restrain the vicious and furnish a fair degree of security and protection by legislation and police control, but the real reform which society in these days is seeking will come as a result of religious convictions, or they will not come at all. Peace, justice, charity – these cannot be legislated into being. They are the result of Divine Grace.[101]

Would that all Americans clearly understood that freedom of religion is the freedom that holds all others together.

Power by Purse Strings

In religious matters, government has evolved from neutrality to antagonism.

We do not have a Church of America, to be sure, but vacuums being abhorred by politicians as well as nature, government has come to embrace a de facto religion called secularism – the anti-religionists – and rejects any whiff of a religious association. The Founding Fathers never would have conceived of the new nation not recognizing its roots and the hand of God in its creation. But that's where our government has arrived.

- It threatens to lift tax exemptions of religions that endorse or oppose a candidate for public office.

- It tells a church in Maryland what type of wedding ceremonies it can and cannot hold on its property.

- Hate-speech regulations are being considered so that a religion cannot preach against sin if such is targeted against a protected group.

- It tells religion-based adoption agencies they cannot restrict adoptions to only those who conform to their religious beliefs.

Government runs a protection racket of sorts. If someone offered to pay you if you would not say certain things, you would tell him to get lost. Same answer if he said you would be fined if you said certain things. You can't be bought, right?

But what if it happened this way: You're told you qualify for a better tax rate than your neighbor and you accept it. Then after you have come to depend on the savings, government comes along and says,

"Nice tax benefit you have here. Would be a shame if you lost it. Tell you what, pal, don't endorse or oppose any political candidates and everything will be okay. Got it?"

Different approach, but this time the bribe works.

That's what government began doing in 1954 with rules against religious ministers endorsing or opposing political candidates from the pulpit, a step toward denying religion a voice in the public square.[102]

Think about it. You can stand on an orange crate on a public street and endorse or oppose whomever you want. But substitute a religious pulpit for the orange crate and you're in trouble.

It's blatantly against the First Amendment, but no one challenged it. The churches caved.

Opposition Strategy

Attacks on religious freedom will not necessarily be head-on; they will be sneaky. Michael Young, president of the University of Washington and past chairman of the United States Commission on International Religious Freedom, identifies three arguments by which enemies of religion seek to dismiss religion's influence through "incremental encroachment," the how-to-boil-a-frog recipe.[103]

> **Argument 1: Religion Is Not Special.** Young says opponents of religion will first argue that "religion is like everything else. It is like a hobby – an interest group with a particular faith [while] somebody else may choose to want to make the highway safe for bicycles. [All activities] are pretty much equivalent." No special place for religion, goes the argument, its front-and-center placement in the pantheon of Creator-given freedoms mere happenstance.

Argument 2: Religion Is Good, But It's a Private Affair. The next argument, Young says, dismisses religion entirely from the public square. He quotes one argument from the Prop 8 dust-up: "Religious participation in the political process can produce dangerous results. Fervent beliefs fueled by suppressed fear are easily transformed into movements of intolerance, repression, hate, and persecution." Sort of like the crazy aunt in the attic: she's your problem; don't let her out on the street.

Argument 3: Religion Has a Negative Impact. Here the opponents of religion go nuclear and liken religions to (gasp) … corporate entities. The argument, as Young analyzes it, holds that "religions, like corporations, are usually motivated by money and power and are prone to socially harmful behavior and misconduct and need to be regulated heavily. Religions endanger social justice, harmony and diversity."

Commonize, privatize, and demonize – a simple three-fold strategy.

Our Position

Short of danger to life and limb when society's authorities must step in, we believe all religions should be left alone to preach as they will and live loyal to those beliefs, proselytize if they choose, take positions on public issues if so inclined, and not be hindered in anything related to religious activity by the smothering hand of government regulations – to be heard in the public square and not just within their houses of worship.

Without a vibrant religious community centered on the belief in and worship of a Higher Being, societies disintegrate.

If freedom of religion as *originally intended* is lost, then deterioration of freedoms of speech, assembly, and press, together with rights to petition government, keep and bear arms, speedy and public trials by jury, due process of law, and protection against self-incrimination, will not be far behind.

We hope many others will join with us in keeping a protective eye on this critically important freedom.

CHAPTER 23

"Mormons Want to Take Over the Government"

How can anyone who mistakenly believes we still practice polygamy possibly think we would have enough time on our hands to take over a government?

Fortunately, only 11% believe this to be our goal. Unfortunately, that's still 26 million people.

Well, we don't practice polygamy and we have as much time as other citizens, but we still don't seek political power.

Besides, how could a church that has both Harry Reid and Glenn Beck as devout members ever agree on a strategy?

Religious Identification

Political junkies and media mavens have been amazed at the extensive publicity the LDS Church has been receiving, most notably because of the presidential candidacies of Mitt Romney and Jon Huntsman.

This attention has tempted some Mormons to bask in the reflected limelight, but I submit the celebration is unwarranted.

While 85% of voters have heard of Mitt Romney, only 41% can identify his religion.

The former Massachusetts governor's two fellow believers on the national scene fare even worse. Only 11% know that Jon Huntsman is a Mormon and an even smaller 6% know that Senate Majority Leader Harry Reid is. Religious identification lags far behind name identification, which means that traits other than religion are driving the penetration into the voters' collective gray matter. The LDS connection isn't sticking as much as expected, except among those who already pay close attention to political contests.

To the extent knowledge of a candidate's religion may impact image or support, however, Romney's religious identification is much higher than that of any other 2012 presidential candidate.

- Barack Obama is identified as a non-affiliated Christian (a safe guess in America) by 29%. Less than 1% identify him with his previous denomination, the United Church of Christ, while 17% still believe he is a Muslim.

- Sarah Palin has shed her Pentecostal and Assembly of God associations, if such had ever really been known, and 27% choose to identify her only, similar to Obama, as a non-affiliated Christian.

- Of the candidates who claim membership in a specific denomination, Michelle Bachmann is correctly tied to her Lutheran religion by 7%, Tim Pawlenty to his Baptist roots by 4%, and Rick Perry to his Methodism by only 1%.

Knowledge of politicians' religions has waned and waxed since our nation's founding, usually in response to particular issues of the day – civil rights, abortion, war – or uniqueness such as Jack Kennedy's

Catholicism (the first Catholic presidential candidate since Al Smith in 1928), or what role Richard Nixon's pacifist Quaker roots would play during his handling of the Vietnam War.

Given that issues with religious overtones are never far away from center ring of the political circus, religious identification will certainly increase for Mr. Romney and Mr. Huntsman as we approach the 2012 election.

Mormons in Politics

Though the presidential candidacy of two Mormons is a first, a Latter-day Saint in politics is not rare. Many may be surprised how many states have sent a Mormon to Congress or to governors' mansions. Our two percent of the population has not been as successful in this field as other low-percentage religions such as Jews and Episcopalians, but the variety of states nonetheless indicates healthy political activity beyond the boundaries of Utah.

If a Mormon were to become president, he would never receive direction from LDS Church leaders

---

- Congress: 11 states have sent an LDS senator or congressman to Washington – Arizona, California, Colorado, Florida, Idaho, Nevada, New Hampshire, New Mexico, Oklahoma, Oregon, and Utah.

- Governors: A Mormon has been a governor of Arizona, Idaho, Massachusetts, Michigan, Nevada, and Utah.

- Cabinet: Mormons have held cabinet positions in various presidential administrations: Agriculture, Education, Health and Social Services, Housing and Urban Development, Interior, and Treasury.

- Outside U.S. borders, Mormons have served in the national legislatures of Brazil, Britain, Canada, Denmark, Japan, Mexico, and Scotland.

Mormon Image: Help or Hindrance?

In 2007, Gallup found that 42% of Americans held a favorable impression of Mormons, while 46% had an unfavorable impression. My February 2008 sampling after Mitt Romney had taken a pounding about his religion, and taken just after he dropped out, had the ratio at 37-49.

The image of Mormons has improved over the last three years, perhaps because of increased visibility, or a greater tolerance from the man on the street toward all religions. Here, from my 2011 poll, are the favorable-unfavorable ratios of six religions, each rated by those not of that faith:

	Favorable	Unfavorable
Baptists	75%	11%
Jews	74	10
Catholics	69	18
Evangelical Christians	53	18
Mormons	48	34
Muslims	40	42

The connection between a religion's image and success in reaching the White House is not very strong. Baptists score highest on favorability of image and claim four presidents: Warren Harding, Harry Truman, Jimmy Carter, and Bill Clinton. Theirs is not a bad correlation with image, although they are underrepresented in the list of presidents proportionate to population. Jews are second, but although they have

Image of Mormons	
Strongly favorable	13%
Somewhat favorable	35
Somewhat unfavorable	19
Strongly unfavorable	15

enjoyed substantial visibility at all levels of government, only one person, Senator Joe Lieberman as a vice presidential candidate, has been nominated to run on a major party's presidential ticket. Catholics are third, but only one has been elected president despite Catholicism being the largest denomination.

If religion were to become a strong determinant of voting preferences, a factor that would have to travel far to upend the economy and foreign policy as voting considerations, the 34% unfavorable rating for Mormons would not bode well for Romney or Huntsman.

Candidate Images

With religious images as background, here are the personal images of certain presidential candidates held by the registered voters in our sample in the summer of 2011:

	Total Recognition	Favorable	Unfavorable
Mitt Romney	85%	52%	25%
Barack Obama	99	48	47
Sarah Palin	97	40	53
Michelle Bachmann	79	36	27
Rick Perry	59	22	18
Tim Pawlenty	56	21	17
Jon Huntsman, Jr.	47	16	12

Pollsters look at the favorable-unfavorable ratio and set a 5:2 ratio or better as the target for their candidates. No candidate reaches this level of strength in this poll, but Romney comes closest in that 52% think well of him compared to 25% who do not.

Which now leads to the question ...

Can a Mormon Be Elected President?

My national poll came at this from three angles: the standard Gallup wording, a three-choice "consider" question, and a projective question that taps how people feel their fellow Americans would vote.

The Standard Approach. The Gallup wording goes like this:

> Between now and the 2012 political conventions, there will be discussion about the qualifications of presidential candidates – their education, age, religion, race, and so on. If your party nominated a generally well-qualified person for president who happened to be _____, would you vote for that person?

When a Mormon candidate is the focus, 80-17 has been the highest Yes-No score, and 72-24 the lowest over the 45 years the question has been asked. The Gallup June 2011 reading was 76-22. I used the same wording in my national poll a month later and the results were 74-16.

Here is how voters in the sample answered this question:

	Yes	No
A Jew	85%	9%
A Catholic	82	10
An Episcopalian	76	11
An Evangelical Christian	75	14
A Mormon	74	16
A gay	56	38
A Muslim	47	44

Pretty much as one might predict. As posed, the question mentions two positive pieces of information usually not mentioned in other measures: (1) that the person has won the nomination of the voter's party, and (2) that he or she is a "generally well-qualified person for president," which contributes to the higher Yes scores. In this approach, the No vote is a firm indicator of rejection for religious reasons because those who want to give a negative answer must swim against a positively phrased question.

Optimism

Of those who would vote for a well-qualified Mormon, 69% can visualize his election and only 23% believe it will not happen.

Of those who would not vote for a well-qualified Mormon, 44% can still visualize his election while an equal number believe it won't happen.

This means that supporters of a Mormon would be more willing to bet that he will be elected than his opponents will bet that he won't.

The Consider Approach. Our second angle was:

I will read you the names of a few religious or other groups in random order. If a person fitting that description or belonging to that religion were running for President, please give me one of three answers regarding your vote …

One… I would definitely consider voting for the person
Two… I might consider voting for the person
Three… I would never consider voting for the person

Here are the results:

	Definitely Consider	Might Consider	Never Consider
A Catholic	50%	41%	4%
A Baptist	47	44	4
A Jew	42	48	6
An Evangelical Christian	42	44	9
A Mormon	30	45	20
A Muslim	19	40	36
An atheist	19	29	48

A three-way answer measures both hard support and hard opposition. Again the top four religions are clustered together with hard opposition in the single digits (it's an axiom of polling that none of those scores will ever be zero). Opposition to a Mormon on this scale is 20%, higher than the 16% cited in the results of the Gallup-wording scenario. Note also that belonging to a particular denomination might have a light-to-moderate impact on a candidate's fortunes, but not believing in God is a poison pill in an election.

The Projective Approach. This technique asks the respondents to think how all Americans might vote. When asked whether they agree or disagree with the statement, "Americans will never elect a Mormon president," the answers reveal deeper attitudes because, the theory goes, people are known to project onto their fellow citizens their own feelings. In other words, voters are more likely to view the world as agreeing with them than disagreeing. The results:

Strongly agree	10%
Somewhat agree	15
Somewhat disagree	35
Strongly disagree	28

Very hard opposition to a Mormon is one out of ten, while an additional 15% reveal an underlying resistance, but will probably wait for an additional reason to vote against him so as not to appear, even to himself or herself, as religiously biased.

Conclusion. An analysis of all three approaches suggests that a Mormon can be elected president, but that he would have to overcome an inherent 7% to 15% bias that candidates belonging to most other religions would not face.

Political Guidelines

So what is the LDS Church's stand regarding all of this?

The LDS Church encourages its members to exercise the right to vote and to make their points of view known – and, if they desire, run for office. But members decide their own level of participation as individuals. The church does not run a political action committee or programs to groom members for public office.

Some worry that if a Mormon were voted into the Oval Office, he would take instructions from Salt Lake, shades of fears during John Kennedy's 1960 campaign and supposed directions from Rome.

Sorry to break up the party, but that will never happen. Elder Quentin L. Cook, a former San Francisco attorney and now an apostle, explained in a TV interview:

> We have a long record in the church of not interfering with public officials, some of whom are members on all sides of almost all public issues. There has been no evidence of any effort to influence that in any way. The members understand that. Political candidates understand that. They don't ever come to the church and say, "What should I do?" [104]

We don't tell politicians what to do, not even our own members who may be elected officials. We would appreciate it if they would return the favor.

Impact of a Mormon President

Split-sample 1: "If a Mormon became president, it would obviously help the image of his church. Would this bother you ... a lot, somewhat, or not at all?"

Split-sample 2: "If a Mormon became president, it would obviously help the image of his church and may cause more people to investigate it and perhaps join. Would this bother you ... a lot, somewhat, or not at all?"

	SS1	SS2
Bother a lot	9%	12%
Bother somewhat	17	17
Bother not at all	72	69

Although most American Mormons today lean toward the conservative side of issues, and tend to vote for Republicans more than Democrats, the church is neutral in matters of party politics.[105] The relationship between members and politics is detailed in the official handbook of instructions given to all local leaders:

- Members are encouraged to participate in the political process and in other causes to improve their nations and communities.

- Members are encouraged to study the issues and vote for candidates of integrity and sound judgment.

- The church is neutral regarding political parties and platforms, and does not endorse any political party or candidate.

- In exceptional instances, the church will take a position on specific legislation in a nonpartisan way, particularly when it concludes that moral issues are involved. If so, only the First Presidency [the President of the Church and his two counselors] will make that decision, not local leaders.

- Members are encouraged to support measures that strengthen the moral fabric of society.

- Members are encouraged to consider serving in public office, but should not imply that their candidacy is endorsed by the church, and may not use church directories or facilities in their campaigns.

No wiggle room. The church is consistently neutral on party politics, even if one of its own becomes a presidential nominee.

In the 2012 campaign, Romney and Huntsman are not Mormon candidates, but rather candidates who are Mormons. In future years, that distinction will hold as well for other contenders who are LDS.

We trust voters will cast their votes for or against any Mormon running for office solely on the merits of issue positions, character, experience, and plans for the country.

CHAPTER 24

"Mormons Will Use Political Power to Force People to Convert"

That 38% of all Americans believe that charge is absolutely baffling.

But then we also found from our study that 37% don't know any Mormons and a majority (54%) do not know an active or devout Mormon, so maybe it's a fear of the unknown.

Mormons began settling the Salt Lake Valley in 1847. As the Gold Rush brought people to the West seeking riches, the LDS Church was the unquestioned dominant political power for 300 miles around. Mormons held every government position, Brigham Young himself was the territorial governor, and we far outnumbered any other religion or group of any kind. If there ever was a time we could have acted on the boogeyman fear cited above, it was in the 1850s.

And what happened? A welcoming hand and no use of political power whatsoever to convert anyone. As other denominations built their churches in Salt Lake, Brigham Young and subsequent leaders of the church offered assistance. Over the years, many Mormon neighbors have participated in building and renovating the cathedrals and sanctuaries of other religions in the city.

That spirit of cooperation continues today, distinct theological differences notwithstanding.

So What Are Mormons Up To?

One of our Articles of Faith says:

> We believe in being honest, true, chaste, benevolent, virtuous, and in doing good to all men; indeed we may say we follow the admonition of Paul – we believe all things, we hope all things, we have endured many things, and hope to be able to endure all things. If there is anything virtuous, lovely, or of good report or praiseworthy, we seek after these things.

Political power is not on the list of things we seek after. And even if we had it, we would never use it to force conversions. That's not the way God does things.

Further, our own scriptures tell us that the church in the last days would have a presence in all areas of the earth, but that its numbers will be few.[106] If God wanted us to force conversions, He would not have given us a minimalist scenario.

Force

"If Mormons had enough political power, they would try to force people to convert."

Strongly agree	16%
Somewhat agree	22
Somewhat disagree	21
Strongly disagree	33

So, in addition to engaging in religious activities such as strengthening members and caring for the poor, what *are* Mormons trying to accomplish? Three things:

- Teach people what we believe is Christ's pure doctrine and invite them to avail themselves of the Lord's sealing power in His temples so their families can be united forever.

- Help people prepare for the Second Coming of Jesus Christ in whatever church they happen to belong.

- Be judged fairly on the facts, and not on what our critics say we believe or do.

Teach People

Jesus Christ told His disciples to go into the world and teach all nations. We believe we hold that same commission today, which is why some 50,000 of our young men and women contribute a prime portion of their youth to tell people what we consider to be the re-established truth.

The church exists to prepare people for eternity

I found that task difficult in the 30 months I spent in Germany as a missionary, but didn't realize until I conducted a series of focus groups a few years ago that it would be difficult even for the Savior.

After finding out what people understood about my church, I concluded each focus group session with this final question:

Let's suppose the event that all of Christianity is looking forward to happened tomorrow – namely, the return of Jesus Christ and the beginning of the Millennium. And let's say He holds a news conference and says point blank that The Church of Jesus Christ of Latter-day Saints, known as the Mormons, is indeed His true, re-established church, and that it is authorized to act in His name and teaches His correct doctrines. What would you do?

A bomb could not have splattered more answers. "I would ask if He's kidding." "I would ask to see His driver's license." "I'd switch channels." "I would still go to my church on Sunday." "I'd go to the beach." "I'd ignore it." "Nothing." And ... "I would join."

Only about three in ten gave that last answer. This was not a quantitative study, of course, and I wonder if we could ever get a truthful measure of this variable short of the actual event, but think what it means at least on the surface: The Lord Himself would have a difficult time convincing a majority of the people to follow Him.

Now, I realize some participants in my groups were being smart alecks and would not act as claimed, but I also came away convinced that many, perhaps a majority, would not change a thing in their lives. They are too comfortable.

Later I turned the question on myself, "What would I do if the roles were reversed and the Savior said, for example, that the Methodists were His true church? Or the Lutherans? Or the Catholics? What would *I* do?"

I doubt I'll be surprised with His announcement on that day for all the reasons I've discussed in this book, but it gave me a good feeling when I answered that I would immediately join whatever church He designated.

I am a follower of Jesus Christ. If He asked me to sit under a Bodhisattva tree and become a Buddhist, I would do it. Or join the Presbyterians. Or the Baptists. Or hand out Hare Krishna flyers at the Los Angeles airport. I would follow His directions.

We are seeking to visit with those 30% who share this same mindset.

Prepare People

Picture this scenario. If you were the writer-producer-director of a play that took thousands of years to present, on a stage as big as the earth, with a cast of billions … what would you do for a finale?

From what Jesus told His disciples, it will be a finale to beat all finales: wars and rumors of war, earthquakes, a world in commotion, men's hearts failing them, seas heaving their bounds, the nations of the world arrayed against Jerusalem, and so on. Maybe even locusts again.

But there's a positive side: Christ's gospel will be preached in all the world, the Jews will return to their homeland and many will accept Him, and the knowledge of God will be spread over the earth (think communication, travel, technology).

The pace is quickening; the world is polarizing.

We believe when that time comes, people will have divided themselves into two camps – the followers of good (who will come from many religions) and the followers of evil. That is why the Second Coming of Jesus Christ is referred to as "a great and dreadful day." Great for those who have done their best and dreadful for those who haven't.

Our job is to maximize the number in the first and minimize the number in the second.

Be Judged on the Facts

Abraham Lincoln once said that if he read, much less answered, the attacks made on him, his office would have to be closed for any other business. He then said:

> If the end brings me out all right, what's said against me won't amount to anything. If the end brings me out wrong, ten angels swearing I was right would make no difference.[107]

We agree with that sentiment. All will be proved in the end.

Meanwhile, we are out in the world trying to explain the commandments and teachings of Jesus Christ as best we know them. It would be nice if we were allowed to defend ourselves on our true positions and not straw-man criticisms.

Image Traits

Mormons are honest

Yes	77%
No	10
No opinion	13

Mormons are pushy

Yes	32%
No	54
No opinion	14

I once conducted a focus group in Colorado for a U.S. Senate candidate and, as the ten or so participants came into the room, I remember thinking that I wouldn't get much useful information from one man about 35 years of age. When it was his turn to introduce himself, he gave an old-fashioned name, I think it was Elmer, and said he was a truck driver. He badly needed orthodontia, had a rooster tail haircut, and had rolled a pack of cigarettes in the sleeve of his yellow T-shirt. Right out of central casting.

On top of that he was shy. After 45 minutes of hearing the other participants discuss a wide range of issues, it became apparent that everyone had spoken except Elmer. So I thought I'd give him his moment in the spotlight and said, "Elmer, you've been quiet. What is your take on what we've been discussing?"

His answer has stayed with me for 25 years. He began, "I have become concerned of late…" (When he said "of late" instead of "lately", I knew his would not be a shallow comment.) "… at the ascendancy of single-issue groups in the nation. If the trend continues, it may well lead to the balkanization of America."

A chair tipped over in the observation room.

The man was well read, conversant on any topic, and as articulate a participant as I have had the pleasure of meeting. From that point on, I did not run the focus group; Elmer did. Every time a participant said anything, he or she would look to Elmer to see if he agreed. It was a boffo performance.

My parents taught me not to judge a book by its cover. Did I ever learn the lesson that night!

We Mormons only ask that people look beyond the false cover painted by our critics and judge us on our actual beliefs, our actions, *our* people.

Epilogue

If I could suggest a few takeaways from the foregoing explanations of the family reunion and the pie fight that would best help you understand Mormons in today's world, it would be these:

- Mormons worship Jesus Christ, the Son of God. They are indeed Christians who believe the Bible.

- Mormons claim that The Church of Jesus Christ of Latter-day Saints is the re-established original Christian church.

- The Mormon nickname applies only to members of the LDS Church. Those who broke away from this church should not be considered Mormons.

- Most American Mormons live outside of Utah, and most Mormons live outside of the United States.

- Mormons do not practice polygamy; it was ended in 1890.

- Mormons believe earth life is Act Two of a three-act play. They believe we lived as spirit children of God before we came here and we will live after we leave. God will judge all of us by what we do and don't do on earth.

- Mormons believe families can be together forever through Christ's sealing power as administered in LDS temples.

- Mormons are productive members of society and work together with many faiths worldwide to alleviate suffering and improve communities.

- Mormons strongly defend freedom of religion on behalf of all faiths.

- Mormons are not a threat. They do not seek political power. They send out 19-year-olds to proselytize, but would never use political force to convert anyone.

- If a Mormon becomes president, he will be accountable to the people of America and will not be given directions from LDS Church leaders.

In the early 1850s, a German professor in Dresden came across an anti-Mormon book.[108] Intrigued by the book's self-contradictions, Dr. Karl G. Maeser began a serious investigation, converted, emigrated to Utah, and became the founder of what is now Brigham Young University, the largest religion-affiliated university in America.

For reasons such as this, we don't mind the jabs at us as long as they do not incite violence as they did in the early days of our church. In fact, I get a kick out of the parodies. As prominent Columbia scholar Richard Bushman observed about the satirical Broadway play about us, "Mormons experience the show like looking at themselves in a fun-house mirror. The reflection is hilarious but not really you."[109]

One person in five has attended a meeting in which a preacher or minister who was not a Mormon talked about the LDS religion, and about half of them felt the lecture contained at least some inaccuracies – the fun-house mirror, as it were. Even though it would be nice if such presentations were more accurate, I hope they continue to argue against us, counterintuitive as it may sound. The more they challenge our claims and our reasoning, the more people will wonder about our side of the story. And many will check out the facts.

I hope you found the answers you were looking for.

Glossary of Mormon Jargon

Adversary – another name for Satan, or Lucifer.

Agency – the power to act for oneself, one of the greatest gifts from God. Sometimes referred to as free agency, free will.

Anoint – to pour a drop of consecrated oil on the head of a person receiving a blessing or a special ordinance.

Anointing oil – a high-grade olive oil consecrated for the healing of the sick and the performance of other ordinances.

Apostasy – the general falling away from the doctrine and practices of original Christianity that accelerated following the death of the apostles.

Apostle – a special witness of Jesus Christ, an office in the Melchizedek Priesthood. The President of the Church, his two counselors, and members of the Quorum of the Twelve Apostles are considered apostles of the Lord Jesus Christ.

Area – a geographic region for administration purposes. The world is currently divided into 26 areas.

Area Authority – a person occupying the office of Seventy with the authority to administer the Church in a specific area. In contrast, a General Authority has the authority to administer the Church anywhere in the world.

Atonement – the sacrifice of Jesus Christ that guarantees resurrection, pays the price of justice and allows our sins to be forgiven, and provides an active power in our lives to enable us to return to God's presence. The most important event in history.

Authority – permission to act in the name of God and Jesus Christ. See *Priesthood.*

Auxiliary – the supplementary organizations for specific member groups: Relief Society, Primary, Young Men, Young Women, and Sunday School.

Baptism – an ordinance for formal entry into membership in the Church at age eight or older. Signifies that the person being baptized has faith, has repented, and is willing to take upon himself or herself the name of Christ. Done by full immersion as a symbol of Jesus Christ's burial and resurrection.

Beehives – a class in the Young Women program for 12- and 13-year olds, also the symbol used to connote industriousness.

Bishop – the presiding officer of a ward (congregation). Usually called for a period of five years. Assisted by two counselors.

Bishopric – the group consisting of the bishop and his two counselors.

Blessing – a formal ordinance using the power of the priesthood on behalf of a person or group. Blessing the sacrament involves set prayers. There is no set prayer in blessings of babies or the sick.

Blessing of a baby – a blessing and naming of a baby a few weeks after birth by those holding the Melchizedek Priesthood. It is usually spoken by the father of the child as he feels inspired.

Blessing of the sick – a two-part blessing on behalf of a person who is sick or in need of special assistance from God. Consists of an anointing first, and then the sealing of the anointing and the blessing as the speaker feels inspired. See *Laying on of hands.*

Block or bloc – the three-hour set of Sunday services consisting of a worship service (sacrament meeting), Sunday school, and then auxiliary and priesthood meetings.

Book of Mormon – a book of scripture, another testament that Jesus Christ is the Son of God.

Branch – a local congregation of members not yet large enough to be organized as a ward. Led by a branch president.

Brother / Sister – forms of address between members, as in Brother Jones or Sister Smith. Derived from the teaching that we are all brothers and sisters because we are children of God.

Calling – an assignment or position.

Celestial kingdom – the highest of three kingdoms of glory in the hereafter, the kingdom where God dwells. The dwelling place for those who were most valiant in following Christ's teachings on earth. The other kingdoms of glory are the terrestrial and the telestial.

Confer – to give or bestow, as in conferring the priesthood on someone.

Confirmation – an ordinance following baptism in which the new member receives the Gift of the Holy Ghost by the laying on of hands.

Consecrate – to bless and dedicate for a special purpose, such as consecrated oil for anointing and blessing the sick.

Convert – one who joins the Church later than age eight.

Covenant – a solemn promise between two parties.

Deacon – an office in the Aaronic Priesthood. Worthy boys as young as 12 years of age may be ordained to this office.

Dedication – the act of dedicating something for a special purpose. For example, we dedicate temples, church buildings, and grave sites.

Deseret – a word from the Book of Mormon meaning honeybee. When Mormons first settled the Salt Lake Valley, they called the name of their state Deseret to signify industriousness.

District – a group of branches not yet large enough to be organized as a stake.

Dispensation – an era of time. Usually identified with a prophet, such as Adam's dispensation or Noah's dispensation.

Dispensation of the fullness of times – if you ever hear this phrase, you will know with 99% certainty that the speaker is a Mormon. It refers to the era of time we are now in, the last dispensation prior to the Second Coming of Christ.

Doctrine and Covenants – a collection of modern-day revelations that we consider scripture, the word of God.

Elder – an office in the Melchizedek Priesthood. A title for both young missionaries and for top hierarchy leaders of the church.

Elders quorum – a priesthood organization at the ward or branch level for adult men who are elders or priests.

Endowment – an ordinance in the temple.

Ensign – a declaration. Also the name of the Church's monthly English-language magazine.

Eternal marriage – marriages that are sealed in the temple and last for eternity, as compared to civil marriages which last only until death.

Eternal progression – the concept that we have always progressed and will continue to progress forever.

Fall of Adam – the transgression of Adam that allowed God's children to experience an earthly or mortal existence. A necessary part of Heavenly Father's plan.

Family history / genealogy – an activity in which members research genealogical records and submit names of ancestors for temple work. The church maintains the world's largest free collection of family history data to which anyone can have access.

Family Home Evening (FHE) – an evening, preferably Monday, set aside for the family to gather together to discuss gospel topics, play games, and for other family-unifying activities.

Fast – to go without food or drink for a period of time, usually two meals, to more purposefully petition God for blessings, and to assist the poor.

Fast offering – a donation to assist the poor, generally calculated on the cost of two meals that members are encouraged to forego once a month.

Fast Sunday – usually the first Sunday of each month.

Fast and testimony meeting – the worship service on Fast Sunday. It does not have designated speakers as on other Sundays, but is given to the bearing of testimonies. Anyone can go to the pulpit and speak to the congregation about his or her testimony.

Firesides – occasional meetings, usually on Sunday evenings, featuring specialty speakers and programs.

First Presidency – the top governing entity consisting of the President of the Church, whom we consider to be God's prophet on earth and the only person authorized to exercise all priesthood keys, and his two counselors.

Garments – sacred clothing worn under street clothes by temple-endowed members.

General Authority – those in the highest hierarchy of Church leadership. Consists of the First Presidency, the Quorum of the Twelve Apostles, the Presidency of the Seventy, the Presiding Bishopric, and the First and Second Quorums of the Seventy.

General Conference – a semi-annual, two-day gathering in Salt Lake City to hear sermons and counsel from general authorities and other top leaders of the Church. Televised to members worldwide.

God – the Father, the Supreme Being we pray to in the name of His Son, Jesus Christ.

Godhead – the ruling triumvirate of the universe, three separate Beings – God the Father, Jesus Christ, and the Holy Ghost. God and Christ possess glorified physical bodies of flesh and bone, while the Holy Ghost is a Personage of spirit only.

Gospel – generally defined as the teachings of Jesus Christ, we also use the term to indicate the totality of Christianity – doctrine, authority, ordinances, organization, and programs.

Grace – the love and tender mercy, a means of help and strength, from God and Jesus Christ. Also, the enabling power of the atonement.

High council – a group of twelve Melchizedek Priesthood holders in each stake who assist and advise the stake presidency.

High priest – an office in the Melchizedek Priesthood.

High priests group – a priesthood organization at the ward level for high priests.

Holy Ghost – the third Member of the Godhead, the teacher and witness of all truth, the Comforter.

Home teaching – a program to foster members helping members. Each family or member is assigned a home teacher who is asked to visit once a month, or more frequently, to discuss gospel teachings and to make sure temporal needs are being met.

House of Israel – descendants of Jacob, who became known by the name of Israel, and was the son of Isaac and the grandson of Abraham. This house has twelve tribes, the Jewish people being of the tribe of Judah. We believe that members of the Church are also part of the House of Israel, mainly through the tribes of Ephraim and Manasseh.

Jehovah – Jesus Christ, the God of the Old Testament.

Jesus Christ – The Son of God, the Messiah. He is the Firstborn of God's spirit children and the Only Begotten Son of God in the flesh. Born of a heavenly Father and Mary, His earthly mother. He is the Redeemer, the Lord, our Mediator, and our Master.

Keys of the priesthood – the authority to direct the priesthood. The priesthood is like a driver's license. One holding it can drive a car, but only with the permission of the person who holds the keys to it. Any priesthood holder except deacons and teachers can perform a baptism, for example, but only upon being directed by the local authority (usually the bishop) to do so. Presiding officers at the stake and ward level hold certain keys, but all priesthood keys are held only by the President of the Church.

Laurels – a class in the Young Women program for 16- to 18-year olds.

Laying on of hands – the act of one or more persons laying their hands on the head of an individual and pronouncing a blessing, conferring a priesthood, ordaining to an office, setting apart a person to a calling, or confirming a newly baptized member.

Line of authority – a document verifying who gave a person the priesthood and from whom that giver himself received it, tracing it back person by person to Joseph Smith who received it from Peter, James, and John, who received it from the Savior Himself.

Lord – generally used to refer to Jesus Christ.

Lucifer – one of God's spirit children who rebelled against God's plan and became the embodiment of evil. Also known as Satan or the adversary.

Meetinghouse – a church building used for Sunday worship services and weekday activities. Also called a church or a ward house.

Messiah – one who saves, the Anointed One. We believe the Messiah is Jesus Christ.

Mia-Maids – a class in the Young Women program for 14 and 15 year olds, a name that originated in a previous Church program known as MIA, or Mutual Improvement Association.

Millennium – although generically a term for any thousand-year period, we use it to designate the thousand years of Christ's righteous rule after His Second Coming.

Mission – usually refers to a calling to spend 12, 18, or 24 months preaching the Gospel or giving specialized service. Also used as a geographic term.

Missionary – one who is called on a mission. Most often applied to 19-23 year old young men and women who serve proselytizing missions.

Mormon – a Christian prophet who lived on the American continent from 310 AD to about 387 AD and who abridged ancient records into what is now the Book of Mormon.

Mormons – a nickname given to members of The Church of Jesus Christ of Latter-day Saints by others because of our belief that the Book of Mormon is scripture that stands alongside the Bible. We did not originate the label, but we answer to it as a convenience and courtesy given the length of our official name.

Moroni – son of Mormon who, as an angel, brought back the ancient records his father abridged and which became the Book of Mormon. A statue of him stands atop many LDS temples.

Mortality – this life we are now in on earth, the life in which we are capable of dying.

Mutual – a shorthand name for the Church's weekday youth program for ages 12 to 18, originally called the Mutual Improvement Association.

Ordinance – a specified procedure or rite conforming to the laws and decrees of God. Baptism, confirmation, marriage, the temple endowment, sealing, and ordinations are among the examples.

Ordain or ordination – giving a person the right to function in a specific office in the priesthood. A person has the priesthood conferred upon him, but an office within the priesthood is received by ordination.

Patriarch – an office in the Melchizedek Priesthood. Patriarchs are chosen from among the especially pure who are most capable of receiving revelation from God for a specific individual. There are only one or two patriarchs per stake.

Patriarchal blessing – a special blessing of guidance and instruction given to worthy members by a patriarch. Often given to members in their teens and considered to be private scripture.

Pearl of Great Price – a selection of canonized materials and ancient transcripts containing points of doctrine.

Plan of salvation – Heavenly Father's plan for the progress, immortality, and eternal life of His children. Also known as the plan of happiness.

Polygamy – the now-forbidden practice of marrying more than one wife, also known as plural marriage. Practiced by commandment by a small percentage of LDS Church members in the 1800s, it was discontinued in 1890.

Pre-existence – shorthand for pre-mortal or pre-earthly existence, the time we lived with God as His spirit children before coming to the earth.

President – one who presides over the Church or a specific entity within the Church, such as an area, mission, stake, district, temple, quorum, auxiliary, or class. In all cases, a president is assisted by two counselors.

Presiding Bishopric – the presidency of the Aaronic Priesthood for the whole Church. Consists of three General Authorities – one designated to be the Presiding Bishop and assisted by two counselors. They are charged with handling the temporal matters of the Church under the direction of the First Presidency.

Priest – an office in the Aaronic Priesthood held by males at least 16 years of age.

Priesthood – the authority and power to act in the name of God and Jesus Christ within the office to which called and ordained. The term is also used to refer to those who hold the priesthood.

Priesthood, Aaronic – the lower priesthood named after Aaron, Moses' brother. Also known as the Levitical Priesthood. Consists of deacons, teachers, priests, and bishops. In almost all cases, a bishop is a high priest functioning as the head of the Aaronic Priesthood in his ward.

Priesthood, Melchizedek – the higher priesthood after the order of the Son of God. To avoid the repetitious use of the Savior's name, it is named after Melchizedek, a great high priest to whom Abraham paid tithes. It includes the offices of elder, high priest, patriarch, seventy, and apostle.

Primary – the organization for children three to twelve years of age. They meet during the second and third hours of our three-hour block of Sunday meetings.

Prophet – the senior apostle of Jesus Christ who is designated to be the President of the Church and receive revelation from the Lord for the whole Church. As President, he is considered to be *the* prophet, but his counselors in the First Presidency as well as members of the Quorum of the Twelve Apostles are also considered prophets. The same office in which Peter served.

Quorum – the organization of each office in the priesthood, such as a deacons' quorum, a priests' quorum, etc.

Relief Society – the auxiliary organization for women, one of the oldest and largest women's organizations in the world, established in 1843.

Restoration – our term for the re-establishment of the original Christian church, as in the phrase, "The Gospel has been restored."

Revelation – specific knowledge, guidance, and commandments given by the Lord. It can happen through visions or audible words, but most often comes through distinct impressions to the mind – a still, small voice. It comes in two forms – prophetic revelation through the prophet to guide the whole Church and maintain doctrinal purity, and personal revelation to each individual to guide his or her own life.

Revelator – one who reveals. The First Presidency and the Twelve Apostles are considered prophets, seers, and revelators.

Sacrament – the Lord's Supper. Consists of bread and water as symbols in remembrance of Christ's sacrifice for us. Through the sacrament we renew the covenants we took upon ourselves at baptism.

Sacrament meeting – our main Sunday worship service in which the sacrament is blessed and passed to the congregation. Held weekly, it consists of prayers, congregational singing, talks by members, and musical numbers. Usually lasts a little over an hour. Visitors from other faiths are welcome to attend and observe; no participation required.

Scriptures – the Bible, Book of Mormon, Doctrine and Covenants, and Pearl of Great Price. Also known as the standard works.

Sealing – a temple ordinance that binds couples together in marriage for time and eternity. Generations are also sealed together, children to parents and parents to children.

Seer – one who sees, who is given to know of events as they will occur. The First Presidency and the Twelve Apostles are considered prophets, seers, and revelators.

Setting apart – a blessing by the laying on of hands that establishes a person in a calling.

Seventy – an office in the Melchizedek priesthood. Seventies have the duty to be special witnesses of Jesus Christ throughout the world.

Single adults – the Church has special wards, organizations, and programs for singles in the Church to facilitate social interaction. In most areas, they are divided into Young Single Adults (18 to 30), Mid-Singles (31 to 45) and Single Adults (over 45).

Sons of Perdition – those who commit the unpardonable sin of denying the divinity of Jesus Christ in the face of perfect knowledge given to them by the Holy Ghost. They will not gain a kingdom of glory.

Stake – an administrative echelon consisting of about six to ten wards and branches. The name originates in the book of Isaiah in which Zion, or the Church, is compared to a tent that is held up by its stakes.

Stake center – a meetinghouse designated to house stake offices as well as wards.

Stake president – the administrative leader of a stake and the presiding officer over the Melchizedek Priesthood in a stake.

Sunday School – doctrinal classes for ages twelve and over, usually held during the second hour of our three-hour block of Sunday meetings.

Teacher – an office in the Aaronic Priesthood given to young men at least 14 years of age. Also someone who teaches a class.

Telestial kingdom – the lowest of the three kingdoms of glory. It is the place where the unrepentant wicked will dwell, but which glory, nonetheless, surpasses all understanding.

Temple – special buildings in which sacred ordinances are performed for the eternal benefit of God's children.

Temple recommend – a noun, not a verb. A certificate verifying that a member is worthy to enter the temple and participate in temple ordinances and worship.

Terrestrial kingdom – the second of the three kingdoms of glory. Those who will receive this kingdom are those who were honorable on earth, but blinded by the craftiness of men.

Testimony – a conviction that something is true. As applied to the Church, it is the faith, the knowledge, and the understanding that God lives, that Jesus is the Christ, and that the church is Christ's authorized, re-established original church. Once a month, the regular weekly worship service (i.e., sacrament meeting) is devoted to the bearing of testimonies, called a fast and testimony meeting, in which one may express this testimony to other members, if desired.

Tithing – an offering of 10% of one's income.

Tracting – a missionary term meaning to knock on doors and hand out tracts, or pamphlets.

Visiting teaching – the Relief Society equivalent of home teaching with the same purposes: to teach and to help.

Ward – a congregation of members. After the family unit, the ward is the next organizational building block of the Church. It usually consists of 300 to 600 members and is demarcated by geographic boundaries. Presided over by a bishop.

Word of Wisdom – our health code that forbids the use of alcohol, tobacco, tea, and coffee. Includes other health recommendations.

Year supply – the Church advises members to prepare for emergencies by setting aside a year's supply of food and other goods.

Young Men / Young Women – the organizations for youth ages 12 to 18. They meet for instruction and activities the third hour of the three-hour Sunday block of meetings and on one evening a week.

Zion – a multiple-definition word that can at turns be the pure in heart, the city of Enoch that was taken into heaven, a place where Christ will return, and the Church in general.

Notes

1 Between July 6 and 13, 2011, Lawrence Research interviewed 1000 adults using random-digit dialing of both land lines and cell phones proportionate to population density in all 50 states. Studies of this size have a margin of error of +/- 3.1 percentage points 95 times out of 100 for mid-range results. The margin of error for the split-sampled questions is +/- 4.5 percentage points. The raw data were weighted on age and education to align with the parameters established by the 2010 census. The wording, sequence, and results may be found at: www.mormonsbelievewhat.com.

2 http://en.wikipedia.org/wiki/Biblical_manuscript.

3 http://pewforum.org/Other-Beliefs-and-Practices/U-S-Religious-Knowledge-Survey.aspx.

4 See chapters 13 and 14 of Zechariah.

5 For this chapter, I have drawn the historical account from *Encyclopedia of Early Christianity*, (Everett Ferguson editor, Garland Publishing, New York, 1988); *The Early Church*, (Henry Chadwick, Penguin, London, 1993); *A Dictionary of Early Christian Beliefs*, (David W. Bercot, editor, Hendrickson Publishers, Peabody, Massachusetts, 1998); *The Influence of Greek Ideas and Usages Upon the Christian Church*, (Edwin Hatch, Williams and Norgate, London, 1895); among other sources.

6 http://www.barna.org/barna-update/article/5-barna-update/82-americans-draw-theological-beliefs-from-diverse-points-of-view.

7   Bart D. Ehrman, professor at the University of North Carolina at Chapel Hill, describes in his book *Misquoting Jesus: The Story Behind Who Changed the Bible and Why*, how the Johannine Comma cannot "be found in the oldest and superior manuscripts of the Greek New Testament [and that it] entered into the English stream of consciousness merely by a chance of history...." (Harper Collins, New York, 2005, 81-82).

8   http://www.newworldencyclopedia.org/entry/Trinity (Please see the 13th paragraph). See also: http://www.wrestedscriptures.com/b08trinity/1john5v7.html

9   http://www.newworldencyclopedia.org/entry/Trinity (Note again the 13th paragraph).

10   John 18:17-27.

11   http://en.wikipedia.org/wiki/Second_Great_Awakening and also http://en.wikipedia.org/wiki/Burned-over_district

12   Joseph Smith History 1:10.

13   Joseph Smith History 1:19.

14   In a vision three years later, an angel named Moroni told Joseph that his name would be had for good and evil throughout the world. That prophecy has come true. Many a youth has claimed he would do some good and great thing, but what teenager would ever think to prophesy he would be known for both good and evil? Perhaps someone who was told so by a heavenly source?

15   Three examples: The scribe during the translation of the Book of Mormon, Oliver Cowdery, also received the priesthood from John the Baptist, and from Peter, James, and John in 1829. In a vision in 1836, Joseph Smith and a counselor in the First Presidency, Sidney Rigdon, saw and conversed with Jesus Christ. Six weeks after that, Joseph Smth and Oliver Cowdery saw in a vision the Savior, followed by Moses, Elias, and Elijah who restored the keys, or special permission, to perform certain work prior to the Second Coming.

16 Revelation 22:18.

17 Of four main interpretive views of Revelation, the Preterist view (that the book is a symbolic history of past events) dates the book to around 70 AD (see http://www.truthnet.org/Christianity/revelation/Introduction/). The claim is that if John wrote Revelation around 70 AD, while the three epistles of John were written between 85 AD and the early 90s (see http://www.abideinchrist.com/messages/1jnintro.html), Revelation would not be the last book John wrote. I consider claims of this sequencing to be inconclusive and only present an interesting possibility. They are, however, not the main reason I maintain that Revelation 22:18 refers only to Revelation and not the whole Bible.

18 In 1 Corinthians 5:9, Paul refers to an earlier letter: "I wrote you in an epistle not to company with fornicators...."

19 The Church's statement on the Broadway musical "The Book of Mormon" is a good example of the perspective we try to carry into a world that is often mocking and derisive: "The production may attempt to entertain audiences for an evening, but the Book of Mormon as a volume of scripture will change people's lives forever by bringing them closer to Christ."

20 Job 38:7 ("When the morning stars sang together, and all the sons of God shouted for joy.") In the New Testament, check out Jude 1:6 (the angels that kept not their first estate – were not obedient in Act 1, the pre-earthly existence) and Revelation 12:4 (a third part of heaven was cast out).

21 Why the difference? In the 2011 study, people were given two mutually exclusive choices. In the Barna study, people were asked to agree or disagree with a two-element description of Satan, thus providing two chances to agree. Mormons believe Satan is a real person as well as a symbol of evil, an option that was not available to respondents in the 1997 study.

22 Revelation 12:7 ("And there was war in heaven; Michael and his angels fought against the dragon; and the dragon fought and his angels.")

23 Isaiah 14:12-16 ("How art thou fallen from heaven, O Lucifer, son of the morning! ...For thou hast said in thine heart, I will ascend into heaven, I will exalt my throne above the stars of God....") See also Luke 10:18.

24 God said to Jeremiah, for example, that He knew him before he was born and, in fact, had already sanctified him and ordained him to be a prophet. (Jeremiah 1:5). In the New Testament, as another example, Paul writes that Christ's disciples were chosen before the foundation of the world (Ephesians 1:4).

25 See http://en.wikipedia.org/wiki/Pre-existence. We know Origen taught this point because he was declared "anathema" in the Fifth Ecumenical Council in 545 AD for doing so because the doctrine evolved for some into a belief in reincarnation. (http://knol.google. com/k/the-reason-why-christians-don-t-believe-in-reincarnation#)

26 William Wordsworth, Poems in Two Volumes, London, Longman, Hurst, Rees, and Orme, 1807. Henry David Thoreau also alluded to the same idea when he wrote, "We now no longer camp as for a night, but have settled down on earth and forgotten heaven."

27 Michael R. Otterson, Director of Public Affairs for the Church, The Washington Post, July 29, 2001. See http://search.earthlink.net/sear ch?q=Michael+Otterson+Washington+Post+cult&area=earthlink-ws &channel=sbt_sgout&abtcgid=87&abtli=0.

28 Sun Tzu, *Art of War.* See http://suntzusaid.com.

29 I served a mission for my church in southern Germany where the last four words of our name do not translate easily into that language. Whereas English speakers say Latter-day Saints, the German translation is *Heiligen der Letzten Tage* – Saints of the Last Days. Such phrasing and syntax invites the addition of adjectives, so for many clever Ger-

mans, the title became Saints of the Last Three Days. I don't know where they came up with the "three," but it sounds apocalyptic – a group of wackos about to announce the date of the end of the world. Obviously their intent.

30 http://www.adherents.com/rel_USA.html#bodies.

31 http://www.fairwiki.org/Jesus_Christ/Worship_different_Jesus.

32 John 20:24-29 and Luke 24:36-43.

33 The sources for these four examples are Matthew 3:16-17, Matthew 26:39, Luke 23:46, and Acts 7:55.

34 http://lds.org/Static%20Files/PDF/Manuals/TheLivingChrist_ TheTestimonyOfTheApostles_36299_eng.pdf Also: James E. Talmage, *Jesus the Christ*, Deseret Book, Salt Lake City, 1915.

35 John 14:6

36 Some maintain that Jesus Christ only taught principles and did not set up a formal organization. This position runs counter to what Paul taught in Ephesians 2:20 that the church was built on a foundation of apostles and prophets, Christ being the chief corner stone, and in Ephesians 4:12 that "he [Christ] gave some, apostles; and some, prophets; and some, evangelists; and some, pastors and teachers." The office of elder is mentioned in Acts 14:23, deacons in Timothy 3, bishops and deacons in Philip 1:1, and the seventy in Luke 10, as examples.

37 http://lds.org/ensign/1998/05/have-you-been-saved?lang=eng/.

38 See *Sons of Perdition* in the glossary.

39 Tad R. Callister, *The Infinite Atonement*, Deseret Book, Salt Lake City, 2000.

40 John 14:15 ("If ye love me, keep my commandments.")

41 The Doctrine & Covenants (D&C) is a collection of modern-day revelations we consider canonized scripture along with the Bible, the Book of Mormon, and the Pearl of Great Price. See Section 76 of the Doctrine & Covenants for a full description of these three kingdoms of glory.

42 In 1 Corinthians 15:40-41, Paul says, "There are also celestial bodies, and bodies terrestrial …" and then refers to three different glories: "There is one glory of the sun, and another glory of the moon, and another glory of the stars…."

43 Here's the reasoning: Jesus said in John 16:15, "All things that the Father hath are mine …" and Paul said in Romans 8:16-17, "… we are the children of God … and joint-heirs with Christ…." Similarly, the Savior told John the Revelator in Revelation 3:21, "To him that overcometh will I grant to sit with me in my throne, even as I also overcame, and am set down with my Father in his throne." As BYU Professor Daniel Peterson has pointed out, isn't it logical that if a=b=c, then a=c? (See http://www.deseretnews.com/article/700168175/Joseph-Smiths-restoration-of-theosis-was-miracle-not-scandal.html.)

44 Matthew 5:48 ("Be ye therefore perfect, even as your Father which is in heaven is perfect.")

45 John 14:2 ("In my Father's house are many mansions … I go to prepare a place for you.")

46 Matthew 6:19-21. Lay not up treasures upon the earth, but lay up treasures in heaven.

47 1 Corinthians 2:9 ("Eye hath not seen, nor ear heard, neither have entered into the heart of man, the things which God hath prepared for them that love him.")

48 Articles such as this one discussing the early Christian prayer circle (maxwellinstitute.byu.edu/publications/transcripts/?id=59) and this one discussing baptisms for the dead (maxwellinstitute.byu.edu/publications/transcripts/?=67) provide many references to the available scholarship on first and second century temple ceremonies.

49 Exodus 30:22-33.

50 1 Corinthians 15:29.

51 Exodus 28 & 29.

52 *The New York Times,* December 6, 2007.

53 In 1990, 22% of Mormons were college graduates; 31% are today, four percentage points above the national average, second only to mainline Protestants among Christian religions. See http://www.americanreligionsurvey-aris.org/reports/ARIS_Report_2008.pdf , page 16.

54 http://yfacts.byu.edu/viewarticle.aspx?id=282 referencing a NORC/ University of Chicago report.

55 Jonah Lehrer, *How We Decide,* Houghton Mifflin Harcourt, New York, 2009, 28-42, 55-56.

56 Lehrer, 1-8, 27.

57 Data from the author's national surveys: 78% of Mormons with at least a college degree attend worship services every week as compared to 56% of Baptists, 43% of Protestants, 37% of Catholics, 23% of non-Christians, and 12% of Jews.

58 Address given to faculty and students of Harvard Law School, February 26, 2010: http://lds.org/ensign/2011/01/fundamental-to-our-faith?lang=eng.

59 Luke 8:10.

60 See Doctrine & Covenants 132:37; Genesis 16:1-11; 25:1; 29:28; 30:4, 9, 26; Exodus 21:10; 2 Samuel 2:2; et al.

61 D&C 132.

62 Official Declaration – 1: http://lds.org/scriptures/dc-testament/od/1?lang=eng.

63 http://www.answers.com/topic/penrose-boies and also http://www.bartleby.com/73/1168.html.

64 D&C 124:49.

65 Official Declaration – 1.

66 http://www.etymonline.com/index.php?search=gender.

67 The Proclamation in its entirety: http://lds.org/library/display/0,4945,161-1-11-1,FF.html.

68 Gordon B. Hinckley, *What Are People Asking About Us?*, Ensign, November 1998.

69 Gordon B. Hinckley, *Why We Do Some of the Things We Do*, Ensign, November 1999, 71.

70 See also Marshall Kirk and Hunter Madsen, *After the Ball: How America Will Conquer Its Fear and Hatred of Gays in the 90's*, Doubleday, New York, 1989.

71 See *Maturation of the Prefrontal Cortex* at: http://www.hhs.gov/opa/familylife/tech_assistance/etraining/adolescent_brain/Development/prefrontal_cortex/index.html   and also http://www.pbs.org/wgbh/pages/frontline/shows/teenbrain/work/adolescent.html.

72 Ephesians 6:5-9. Paul, sensitive to being seen as an insurrectionist, told servants, bond and free, to "be obedient to them that are your masters according to the flesh..." and admonished masters to forbear threaten

73 This series of quotes begins with D&C 101:79 followed by Mosiah 27:3; 2 Nephi 26:38; D&C 38:25; D&C 38:27; D&C 51:9; D&C 78:6; and D&C 38:16.

74 D&C 36:4-5. The only group that is specifically denied the priesthood in the scriptures are those who participated in mob activities against the church (D&C 121:21).

75 Executive Order 44; State of Missouri; Lilburn W. Boggs, Governor; October 27, 1838. Rescinded June 25, 1976 by Governor Christopher S. Bond.

76 Brigham Henry Roberts, *The Rise and Fall of Nauvoo*, Deseret Book, Salt Lake City, 1900, 54.

77 In 1870, Mormon-dominated Utah was the second state (Wyoming was first) to grant women the right to vote. This was a full 50 years before the 19th Amendment gave this right to all women in America. http://en.wikipedia.org/wiki/Women's_suffrage_in_Utah.

78 In 1954, the Supreme Court in *Brown v. Board of Education* overturned the doctrine of "separate but equal" given in *Plessy v. Ferguson* in 1896. Ten years later, Congress passed the Civil Rights Act of 1964, which was followed in 1965 by the landmark Voting Rights Act.

79 Official Declaration 2 of The Church of Jesus Christ of Latter-day Saints, June 8, 1978, unanimously sustained in General Conference September 30, 1978.

80 Marvin Perkins, *Blacks in the Scriptures* (DVD): "The beauty of the revelation is that it gave us so much more light and knowledge."

81 Elder Bruce R. McConkie, an apostle, stated, "Forget everything that I have said, or what President Brigham Young or President George Q. Cannon or whomsoever has said in days past that is contrary to the present revelation. We spoke with a limited understanding and without the light and knowledge that now has come into the world." (August 18, 1978: See http://speeches.byu.edu/reader/reader.php?id=11017.

82 Gordon B. Hinckley, *Ensign*, May 2006, 58. See http://ldsorg. churchmagazines/5-2006-Ensign/May2006Ensign.pdf.

83 Darius Gray, *Blacks in the Scriptures (DVD)*.

84 *The Salt Lake Tribune*, November 4, 2004.

85   Hinckley, 58.

86   Personal letter from Marvin Perkins.

87   Heber J. Grant, General Conference, Salt Lake City, October 1936.

88   University of Tennessee law professor Glenn Reynolds put it this way: "But home ownership and college aren't causes of middle-class status, they're markers for possessing the kinds of traits – self-discipline, the ability to defer gratification, etc. – that let you enter, and stay, in the middle class. Subsidizing the markers doesn't produce the traits."

89   The Family: A Proclamation to the World; The First Presidency and Council of the Twelve Apostles; Salt Lake City, September 23, 1995.

90   D&C 121:37.

91   http://www.beliefnet.com/resourcelib/docs/21/Benjamin_Franklins_Request_for_Prayers_at_the_Constitutional__1.html.

92   http://www.lextek.com/clark/10890.html.

93   Pew Research Center, Forum on Religion & Public Life, 2009.

94   C.F. Adams, *The Works of John Adams*, Little, Brown and Company, Boston, 1969, 228-229.

95   To the Executive of New Hampshire, November 3, 1789, Writings 30:453.

96   P.L. Ford, ed., *Essays on the Constitution*, Historical Printing Club, Brooklyn, New York, 1892, 251-52.

97   Federalist 37.

98   Ether 2:12.

99   Brian J. Grim and Roger Finke, *The Price of Freedom Denied; Religious Persecution and Conflict in the Twenty-First Century*, Cambridge University Press, New York, 2011, 3-10.

100 Dallin H. Oaks, Chapman University, Orange, California, February 4, 2011. Transcript: http://newsroom.lds.org/article/elder-oaks-religious-freedom-Chapman-University.

101 Speech at the unveiling of the equestrian statue of Bishop Francis Asbury, 15 October 1924, Washington, D.C. See http://www.god-and-country.info/CalvinCoolidge.html.

102 In the summer of 1954, Senator Lyndon B. Johnson proposed a change in IRS rules, a change that has become known as the Johnson Gag Order. The chief clerk of the Senate read the change: "On page 117 of the House bill, in section 501(c)(3), it is proposed to strike out … 'influence legislation' and insert 'influence legislation, and which does not participate in, or intervene in (including the publishing or distributing of statements), any political campaign on behalf of any candidate for public office.'" The measure passed on a voice vote. See: http://stkarnick.com/culture/2011/04/14/the-silence-of-the-shepherds-landslide-lyndon-the-irs-and-the-big-chill-they-continue-to-work-on-churches/.

103 http://newsroom.lds.org/article/protecting-religious-freedom and http://www.deseretnews.com/article/700124424/University-of-Utah-President-Michael-K-Young-says-religious-freedom-on-defensive.html.

104 http://www.youtube.com/watch?v=0S6cW-o0oTg.

105 See the full statement on political neutrality at: http://newsroom.lds.org/official-statement/political-neutrality.

106 1 Nephi 14:12.

107 http://rogerjnorton.com/Lincoln78.html.

108 Moritz Busch, *Die Mormonen* (The Mormons).

109 http://inthearena.blogs.cnn.com/2011/06/richard-bushman.